HAMPTON HISTORY

HAMPTON HISTORY

AN ACCOUNT OF THE PENNSYLVANIA HAMPTONS IN AMERICA IN THE LINE OF

JOHN HAMPTON, JR.

OF WRIGHTSTOWN

WITH AN APPENDIX TREATING OF SOME OTHER BRANCHES

BY

JOHN HAMPTON DOAN

TEACHER AND MINISTER

ISBN: 978-93-5128-725-4(HB)

First Published in 1911
Indian Reprint in 2017

Published by

Kalpaz Publications
C-30, Satyawati Nagar,
Delhi – 110052
E-mail: kalpaz@hotmail.com
Website: kalpazpublications.com
Ph.: +91-9212142040

Cataloging in Publication Data—DK
Courtesy: D.K. Agencies (P) Ltd. <docinfo@dkagencies.com>

Doan, John Hampton, 1828- **author.**
Hampton history : an account of the Pennsylvania Hamptons in America in the line of John Hampton, Jr., of Wrightstown : with an appendix treating of some other branches / by John Hampton Doan.
pages cm
"First published in 1911"—Title page verso.
ISBN 9789351287254 (HB)

1. Hampton family. 2. Hampton, John Jr., 1763-1842. 3. United States—Genealogy. I. Title.

CS71.H23D63 2017 DDC 929.373 23

INTRODUCTION

THE living members of the Hampton family in America and their relatives represented in this history have good cause to be thankful. They are a favored people, both because of a worthy ancestry; and because there were those among that ancestry who were intelligent enough and altruistic enough to make and preserve family records sufficient for an outline history of the family going back in an unbroken line about 200 years, to their first ancestor in America. Herein is a stimulus toward noble living for our young people, not possessed by some families.

If the making of this book should impress on the minds of those interested in it, the importance of making records it will result in good not anticipated.

The sources of the historical matter contained in this book are chiefly the following:

1. The accounts of her life, her kindred and relatives and their homes, given by my mother, Asenath Hampton Doan, to her children, much of which was treasured up in my memory.

2. The records in the family bible of John and Mary Betts Hampton.

3. Personal association in early life with my grandfather, John Hampton, and with several of the fourth and fifth generations.

4. A written record of her parents' family and other kindred and relatives made and given to me by my mother at my request many years ago.

5. A letter in answer to inquiries sent me by my aunt, Mary Ann Robins, in 1889.

6. Dr. E. D. Buckman's papers of Doan history in which

he traces the genealogy of Asenath Hampton because she had married a Doan.

7. A record made by John Hampton, of Viola, Iowa, similar to that of his sister, Asenath, and loaned me by his daughter, Anna.

8. A very large portion has been secured by laborious correspondence, extending over a period of five years with persons of the fifth and sixth generations.

The writing required in this correspondence, together with the arranging of the matter and then making a final copy for the printer, was all done after the writer was seventy-six years of age, and without the aid of glasses, except the occasional use of a lens or "reading glass."

Immense labor and care has been taken to secure accuracy in everything and yet such is the ease with which mistakes may be made in copying figures, that it is too much to hope that no error will be found.

Two errors in dates have already been detected in the writing of correspondents and corrected.

The work is one of love and good will and was done without expectation of pecuniary rewards.

The Author.

West Carrollton, Ohio.
July, 1910.

Origin of the Pennsylvania Hamptons in America.

TRADITION.

There is a tradition in this branch of the Hampton family in America that three brothers of the name of Hampton came from England and settled in three different states.

This is as I remember hearing my mother, Asenath Hampton Doan, relate it in my childhood, except that she named Pennsylvania as one and was not so positive about the other two states.

But my brother, James Doan, had it four, instead of three of them, and that there were two sets of children by the same father, two being half brothers to the other two and that they settled in four different states, and thought he had this direct from our grandfather.

It is certain that grandfather believed that the South Carolina Hamptons were of the same stock as the Pennsylvania Hamptons.

HISTORY.

1 "JOSEPH HAMPTON, from England, married Mary Canby," about September, 1722. He was born probably in the last decade of the seventeenth century, 1690 to 1700.

"Mary Canby, his wife, was born the 12th of the 9th month, 1697, and died the 4th of the 8th month, 1794, and was buried at Wrightstown" aged nearly ninety-seven years.

In the above statement about Joseph Hampton and Mary Canby, the sentences inclosed in quotation marks are copied literally from the family records and together with the names of their children to be copied below, constitute all that for a long time was known to the decendents of John and Mary Betts Hampton about our great ancestor and his wife.

The following interesting items about Joseph Hampton, the progenitor of the Pennsylvania Hamptons, I obtained from Dr. E. D. Buckman, of Philadelphia, who in gathering materials for a history of the Doan family, also spent some labor in tracing the lineage of my mother, Asenath Hampton, because she had married a Doan. His statement is substantially as follows:

"The exact time of his coming to America or to Wrightstown, is not yet discovered, but the records of Buckingham Monthly Meeting show that he made public declaration of marriage with Mary Canby on the 9th day of the 8th month, 1722.

"Joseph became the ancestor of the Bucks County Hamptons and his posterity is widely scattered over the northern states of this Union, though many of them remain denizens of Bucks County.

"Dr. Charles W. Smith, in his brief history of the first settlement of Wrightstown, relates that Joseph Hampton came there in 1724, and purchased of Zebulon Heston, 250 acres, a part of the Richardson tract. This adjoins the Doan's tract on the south. This tract or a large portion of it has descended to Moses Hampton, who as late as 1876, was owner of it.

"Joseph Hampton was an active business man, an exemplary member of society and did much to encourage improvements. He built what has long been known as the Anchor Tavern and for many years kept a public house for the entertainment of travelers."

Dr Buckman also gives a diagram of Asenath Hampton's lineage in which he shows that Mary Canby was the daughter of Thomas Canby, born in England, in 1667, and

Sarrah Jarvis Canby, of Abington, his wife, whom he married, 1683-9-2.

In speaking of Joseph Hampton's declaration of marriage with Mary Canby, Dr. Buckman adds, "Her father, Thomas Canby, in the same meeting, and on the same day, declared his intention of marriage with Mary Jane Bestam who became his third wife."

Children:

2 I BENJAMIN.

3 II JOHN b, 12th of 1st month, 1724.

III SARAH, who married a Wilson.

IV MARY, who married James Stokes.

Second Generation

2 BENJAMIN (2) HAMPTON (Joseph 1) born probably in 1723, and died probably in 1815. He lived to be niney-two (92) years old and died sitting in his chair. He was in the habit of taking a nap after dinner, sitting in a chair, and so it happened his dying was not noticed by the family.

I have this statement about his age and death from my mother. He married Ann Wildman.

Children:

7 I BENJAMIN, Jun.
8 II OLIVER.
9 III JAMES.
IV MARY, who married Dr. John Watson.
V ANN, who married Joseph Duer.
VI ELIZABETH, who married Joseph Coleman.

3 JOHN (2) HAMPTON, (Joseph 1) born the 12th of 1st month, 1724, died 10th of 9th month, 1775.

He married Ann Croasdale daughter of Jeremiah and Grace (Heaton) Croasdale, who was born the 18th of the 11th month, 1730. Both Grace Croasdale and her daughter, Ann Croasdale Hampton, were approved ministers of the gospel among the Friends.

Children of John (2) Hampton and Ann Croasdale:

4 I ASENATH, born 15th of 11th month, 1749.
5 II SARAH, born 3rd of 10th month, 1751.
10 III JOSEPH, born 17th of 8th month, 1753.

IV HANNAH, born 6th of 7th month, 1756, died same year, 12th month, 25th.

11 V DAVID, born 24th of 10th month, 1757.

12 VI JONATHAN, born 2nd day of 9th month, 1760.

16 VII JOHN, born the 18th day of the 10th month, 1763.

6 VIII ANN (3), born 3rd of 4th month, 1767.

Daughters of This Family and Their Children:

4

ASENATH (3), (John 2, Joseph 1), married Isaac Comly. Their children were: 1 Martha, 2 John, 3 Isaac, 4 Joseph, 5 Ezra, 6 Ethan, 7 Jason.

JOHN COMLY, the second child and oldest son, was the most noted descendent of the original Joseph Hampton, that had appeared in his day.

He was an approved minister and teacher among the Friends and eminent in both positions. His name is in the list of teachers in the Westtown school, the oldest and most noted of the Friends schools in America, having entered as teacher (or principal) 1800-6-11, and retired in 2nd month, 1802.

He was the author of an elementary English Grammar, much used among the Friends and noticed by Gould Brown in his "Grammar of English Grammars."

A large book has been published entitled "Life and Religious Work of John Comly."

5

SARAH (3) HAMPTON, (John 2, Joseph 1) second daughter and second child of John and Ann Croasdale Hampton, married Isaac Smith.

Their children's names were: Eber, Hannah, Sarah, David, Isaac, Asenath, Jonathan and Rachel.

6

ANN (3) HAMPTON, (John 2, Joseph 1) youngest child and daughter of John and Ann Croasdale Hampton, married John (or Jeremiah) Livsey. Their children were: Asenath, John, Samuel, Jesse and Jason. John Livsey, the oldest son married Sarah Roman, a woman of beautiful Christian character, and moved to Ohio.

He lived on Goshen Run, near Wolf Creek, about two miles from Chesterfield (Postoffice Chester Hill) Marion township, Athens, now Morgan Co., O.

He was a man of note in his neighborhood. Was township trustee and was once appointed as "Viewer," to help lay out a state road authorized by the legislature.

Later in life he left his farm (a good one) and lived in Chesterfield. His children were: Oliver, Hannah Ann, Jesse, Jeremiah and Lovina. Oliver married Elizabeth Boswell in Chesterfield and lived there a while but died early. Hannah Ann married Daniel Mott, and lived a few miles south of Plymouth, Washington Co., O. Had no children. Good people.

Jesse went to Belmont Co., O., and lived near Barnesville. Married Elizabeth Patterson, had several children. He was in California in 1905, a bright, good man. Two of his children, Charles Livzey and Anna (Livzey) Hall, were living near Barnesville, O., in 1905.

Jeremiah, a pleasant boy, injured himself plowing a field of heavy limestone clay soil. He lingered in poor health, did some painting in an amateur way, very creditably. Later he was able to do some work but his mind became effected and he spent the latter part of his life in the Athens, Ohio, Insane Asylum.

Lovina married Joseph Boswell, a brother of Elizabeth, who had married Oliver; went to California; husband died and she married a Hall(?) and lived in Pasadena in 1905.

After the death of the elder Livzey, the mother, Ann Hampton Livzey, and some of the other children moved to Ohio about 1839 or 1840. Asenath, Samuel and Jason, I believe, came with the mother; all unmarried. All but Samuel returned to Pennsylvania. He married Rebecca King, a daughter of James King, of Penn Township, Morgan Co., Ohio. About the time of the rebellion in the sixties of the last century he moved to Troy Township, Athens Co., Ohio, and became a near neighbor of his cousin, Asenath Doan. Samuel and Rebecca Livzey's children were: (1) James, (2) Thomas, (3) John, (4) Ann, (5) Lewis, (6) Samuel, (7) Martha,(8) Emmor and (9) Sarah.

Third Generation

7

BENJAMIN (3) HAMPTON, JR., (Benjamin 2, Joseph 1) married MARY POWELL (or POWNELL.)

Children:

I MOSES. It seems quite possible he was the ancestor of Benjamin Bowles Hampton, the editor of Hampton's Magazine, but it is also quite possible that Oliver's son, Charles, may have been so, instead of Moses. (See Appendix).

II SARAH.

III BENJAMIN. Married Hannah Morris and became the ancestor of the Jersey Hamptons, who had their seat originally at Quakertown, Hunterdon Co., N. J.

IV JOSEPH. It seems highly probable that this is Joseph Hampton, born about 1785, who married Mary Rummidge and became the ancestor of the Utah Hamptons. (See Appendix).

V HANNAH.

VI MARGARET.

VII MARY. (Twin of Ann VIII).

VIII ANN. (Twin of Mary VII).

IX CATHARINE. (See Appendix).

8

OLIVER (3) HAMPTON, (Benjamin 2, Joseph 1) married first,———; second, Margaret Kitchen, John Kitchen's widow. Their son's name was Charles. Oliver and his brother James (named next below) had the reputation of being the best penmen and scholars about Wrightstown.

9

JAMES (3) HAMPTON, (Benjamin 2, Joseph 1) was a school teacher many years and died unmarried.

10 JOSEPH (3) HAMPTON (John 2, Joseph 1) born 1753-8-17, married Mary Baker and settled in Catawissa.

Children's names: Mary, David, John, Joseph, Abner, Samuel, Hannah, Amos, Jonathan, Ann and Noah.

11 DAVID (3) HAMPTON, (John 2, Joseph 1) born 1757-10-24, married Rebecca Phillips, daughter of Aaron Phillips.

Their children were: Joseph, Mary and Mercy.

Whether any of this family moved to Ohio is not known to the writer, but a "Public Friend," (Quaker preacher) who was a cousin to Asenath Hampton Doan, visited her in Athens Co. Ohio, in the fall of 1850, who it seems likely was this Joseph.

12 JONATHAN (3) HAMPTON, (John 2, Joseph 1) born 1760-9-2, married 1783-4-13, Elizabeth Phillips, born 1762-7-25; he died 1832-10-10; she died 1843-5-30.

Children:

13 I THOMAS, born 1784-2-7.
II ELI, born 1787-7-13, died 1855-7-12.
III REBECCA, born 1790-5-12.
14 IV MARY, born 1792-9-24.
V ELIZABETH, born 1797-9-1. Married to —— Mendenhall.
VI JONATHAN, born 1797-10-15.
VII AARON, born 1804-2-23.

Part, and perhaps all, of this family moved to Ohio.

13 THOMAS (4) HAMPTON, (Jonathan 3, John 2, Joseph 1) born 1784-2-7 in Pennsylvania (?) and died in Ohio (?) 1827-7-12, married Hannah Roman, daughter of Abraham Roman.

Childrens names were: Cary, Eunice and Jason. The family lived in 1836 and later between Pennsville and Chester Hill in Morgan Co., Ohio.

14 MARY (4) HAMPTON, (Jonathan 3, John 2, Joseph 1) born 1792-9-24, married to Isaac Roman, 1813-4-28, son of Abraham and Hannah Roman and born 1788-6-29.

Children:

I EPHRIAM ROMAN, born 1814-8-1, married Ann T. John, 1838-9-20, in Chesterfield, Morgan Co., O. Children: 1 Rachel, 2 Isaac, 3 Mary Jane, 4 Jesse, 5 William, 6 Amos, 7 Eli H., 8 Elwood D., 9 Sarah Elizabeth. They lived near Plymouth, Washington Co., O.

II EZRA ROMAN, born 1816-4-21.

III SARAH ANN ROMAN, born 1818-4-19.

IV AMOS ROMAN, born 1820-8-23.

V HAMPTON ROMAN, born 1823-3-27.

VI ABRAHAM ROMAN, born 1827-2-12.

VII ELIZABETH H. ROMAN, born 1831-9-30. A pleasant, Christian woman. Did not marry. Lived at the old ladies home in Marietta, O., the latter part of her life.

Mary and Isaac Roman after going to Ohio, lived first at Blue Rock, Muskingum Co., later in Morgan and Athens Counties.

15 CARY (5) HAMPTON, (Thomas 4, Jonathan 3, John 2, Joseph 1). Married Sarrah Way in Chesterfield, (now Chester Hill) Morgan Co., O., about 1838. (?)

Lived at Southland, a few miles from Plymouth, Washington Co., O.

Children:

I ELVINA, who married Wm. Hoyle and lived a few miles from Viola, Ia., in 1905.

II THOMAS, married and had several children.

III HANNAH ANN, unmarried.

THE BETTSES AND CARYS.

Before treating of the history of the remaining member of the family of John and Ann Croasdale Hampton, it will be well to have some account of the Betts family, of Bucks Co., and also of the Cary family, whose blood mingled in the veins of Mary Betts, whom he married. These are our ancestors equally with the Hamptons. According to my mother's account, the Bettses were originally from Wales.

THOMAS BETTS, of Long Island, married Susannah Field, in New Jersey, and settled in Bucks Co., Pennsylvania.

Their Children:

I THOMAS.
II MERIAN.
III STEPHAN.
IV SUSANNAH.
V MARY.
VI DAVID.
VII PATIENCE.
VIII RICHARD.
IX ZACHARIAH.
X WILLIAM.
XI JOHN.

This list is according to Asenath Hampton Doan's record. Her brother, John Hampton, had a record with the same names, except John but were in a different order and substituted Mary Ann for John.

ZACHARIAH (2) BETTS, (Thomas 1) married 1st, Rachel Bye, had one child, Jesse. Married 2nd, Bethula Cary, children, Mary, Mirian, Samuel. Married 3rd Mary Lacy, children 1 Esther, 2 Mercy, 3 Thomas, 4 Rachel, 5 Susannah, 6 Joseph and 7 Zachariah.

JESSE (3) BETTS, (Zachariah 2, Thomas 1) married Hannah, daughter of Aaron Paxton. Children's names were: Benjamin, Rachel, Deborah, Mahlon and Charles.

MARY (3) BETTS, (Zachariah 2, Thomas 1) born in Upper Markfield, Bucks Co., the 26th day of 7th month, 1771, married John Hampton, of Wrightstown, the 20th day of 6th month, 1787.

She became the mother of twelve children. Her further history will be given in connection with that of her husband and their family.

MIRIAM (3) BETTS, (Zachariah 2, Thomas 1) married Joseph Lownes, son of William and Mary Lownes, of Upper Markfield. Their children: Charles, Bethula, Rebecca, Mary Ann, Josiah, Esther, Zachariah and William. Esther Lownes lived many years and died unmarried. "A worthy woman."

SAMUEL (3) BETTS, (Zachariah 2, Thomas 1) married Grace Kirkpatrick. Their children's names were: Zachariah, Mary L., Hannah K., Richard K., William C., Alice Eliza and Sarah.

I have no record of the marriages of the third wife's—Mary Lacy's—children.

The descendents of this Betts family have for many years been residents of Philadelphia, and reputed to be very worthy people.

SAMUEL CARY, "of English origin and dignity," married Sarah Stackhouse.

Children:

Asenath Doan's record:

I SAMPSON.
II SAMUEL.
III ANN.
IV MARY.
V ASA.
VI SARAH.
VII BETHULA.
VIII BEULA.
IX HEPSIBA.

John Hampton's record:

I SAMPSON.
II SAMUEL.
III ANN.
IV SARAH.
V HANNAHMEEL.
VI JOSHUA.
VII MARY.
VIII THOMAS.
IX BETHULA.
X BEULA.
XI HEPSIBA.

Ann married Manuel Walker and settled in Philadelphia, Penn.

Sarah married William Blakey, of Middletown, Pa.

Mary married Joshua Canby, also of Middletown.

Bethula married Zachariah Betts.

"Sarah Cary, nee Stackhouse, and her son-in-law, William Blakey or Blakley, were eminent ministers of the gospel in the society of Friends." The Carys were of the "gentry" class in England and brought with them to America, their "Coat of Arms," which it was common for wealthy and aristocratic families to have in England.

The Carys and Bettses became related by the marriage of Bethula Cary, daughter of Samuel, from England, with Zachariah (2) Betts (Thomas) as his second wife. And these two families became related to the Hamptons by the marriage of MARY BETTS, oldest child of this Zachariah Betts and Bethula Cary with

16 JOHN (3) HAMPTON, (John 2, Joseph 1) b, 1763-10-16, She was born in Upper Markfield, Bucks Co., Penn., the 26th day of the 7th month, 1771. This marriage took place the 20th of 6th month, 1787, when the bride was not quite sixteen years old. The Betts family were opposed to the marriage. Whatever other causes there may

have been, the youthfulness of the bride must have been one.

John Hampton, the bridegroom was a young school teacher. Because of the opposition of the parents of the bride, they could not be married in the mode of the Friends and decided to be married by a justice of the peace. But the law required a notice or "publication of the bans," so our grandfather hit upon the plan of having a friend of his, follow closely on the heels of the poster of the notices and read them (three I believe) and then pull them down and destroy them. In this way he had a witness to prove that the lawful notice had been posted and also had been seen and read and yet the word of the coming wedding did not reach the ears of the bripe's parents till after the marriage. It is hard to fence against cupid.

Dr. Buckman says: "John (Hampton) married 1788, 2nd month, 4th, (this date is probably an error) with Mary Betts, and in doing so disregarded the discipline of the society of Friends and was disowned for that act."

If they were disowned as it seems not unlikely they both were, they must have been reinstated for the children all seem to have had a "birth right" in the society.

But the Betts family evidently became reconciled whether the church did or not, for the bride was helped to an outfit for house-keeping, some items of which continue to exist to the present time. Grandmother (Mary Betts Hampton) at her death bequeathed to my mother (Asenath Hampton Doan) a heavy silver spoon, it being one of a set, or half set, given to her by her father with the letters "M. B." engraved on the handle; and because she was named for her grandmother, my mother gave it to my sister, Mary, who still holds it, 1907, as an heirloom. Another of these spoons is still in existence in Iowa.

Also our great grandfather, Zachariah Betts, was a carpenter and joiner and after this marriage, he had a large chest made in his shop, in the then current style, in a very neat and substantial manner, with a till at one end and with a lid on it and a secret drawer under it. That old chest, well preserved, was in my father's and mother's old home in Athens Co., O., late in the nineteenth century.

Moreover, I have heard my mother tell of her visits in childhood to her grandfather Betts', and of his pleasant home on the banks of the Delaware.

Beside help to begin housekeeping, our great grandfather, gave his daughter, Mary a large family Bible. It was in this wise. An edition of the Bible was to be published in America if subscribers enough could be obtained. Zachariah Betts subscribed for one dozen. He had eleven children and one dozen would supply one for each child and one for himself.

My mother said this was the first edition of family Bibles published in America (perhaps it should have been Pennsylvania.) The copy of the Bible given to Mary B. Hampton, is still in existence (Jan., 1906) in possession of Anna Hampton, Springville, Iowa., and contains valuable records.

Children of John and Mary Betts Hampton:

17 I CARY, born the 4th of 5th month, 1788.
18 II JESSE B., born the 21st of 7th month, 1789.
19 III BETHULA B., born 1st of 8th month, 1791.
20 IV JAMES, born 26th of 6th month, 1794.
21 V ASENATH, born the 3rd of 3rd month, 1796.
22 VI ZACHARIAH, born the 25th of 1st month, 1798.
23 VII ASA C., (CARY?) born 7th of 5th month, 1800.
VIII SARAH G., born the 26th of 3rd month, 1802, and died the 24th of 7th month, 1808.
24 IX JOHN, born the 26th of 2nd month, 1806.
25 X SAMUEL B., born 9th of 4th month, 1809.
26 XI MARY ANN, born 1st of 2nd month, 1811.
27 XII CARY, 2nd, born the 17th of 7th month, 1814.

Whether their first home after marriage, was at Wrightstown, is not certain but seems probable. It is on record that their daughter, Asenath, was born there and that later they moved into the adjoining township of Middletown, near Newtown. From there the family moved in 1801, to Montgomery county, Maryland, and settled at a place called Sandy Spring, fourteen miles from Washington City. The older sons and perhaps the father, used to take marketing to Washington City.

In 1808, they moved to Fredrick Co., Maryland, and settled about four miles from New Market, and thirty-four from Baltimore.

They held their church membership with the Society of Friends, at a place called Bush Creek, which appears to have been near New Market. Their monthly meetings I believe were also there. Their quarterly meeting was at a place called Pipe Creek. Pipe Creek is a branch of the Monocacy river, and is north of New Market. Their yearly meeting was at Baltimore, which is a little south of east and distant about 30 miles from New Market. The Yearly Meeting owned a piece of land outside of the city where the horses of members from the country were pastured and cared for during the sessions of the meeting, while their owners were provided for by Friends in the city. Members of the family often attended these meetings.

The family home then consisted of what Uncle John calls "a fine fruit farm of 190 acres." I have many times heard my mother (Asenath Hampton Doan) tell of the fine fruits they had there especially cherries and apples. But such fruit, though so valuable now, at that day, thirty-four miles from a city and no railroads, would not be of much money value, however much health and comfort it might bring to the family. Two things seem to have conspired to cause their removal to Ohio. The only one assigned by Uncle John is that Maryland was a slave state. This to them, was a serious cause of dissatisfaction during all their sojourn of twenty-four years in Maryland. The other cause was an incumbrance on the land they could not remove. In the spring of 1825, after seventeen years in Frederick Co., and twenty-four in the state, they removed to Ohio, whither the oldest unmarried son, Zachariah, had preceeded them the year before to select a new home for them.

Their oldest living son, James, and the only married

one of the family then, (Jesse having been dead over ten years) was living in Pennsylvania. He brought his little family consisting of a wife and two children, the younger only about six weeks old, down to the old home in Maryland, and came west with the rest of the family. They started about the first of May and came into Belmont Co., Ohio., where Zachariah had first located near Flushing, having been married barely a month.

There or not far from there, James and his family also located. But Zachariah soon moved on into Morgan Co., near Pennsville. The parents and most, if not all the rest of the family, proceeded on west and south into Muskingum Co., and settled in Blue Rock township, near the Morgan Co. line and near the present village of Ruraldale. In the neighborhood, at that day, there was a small settlement of Friends.

They had left behind them, in Maryland, a little grandson, Jesse Hampton, Jr., about ten years old, and his mother, their widowed daughter-in-law and three children, in their graves. Little Sarah, six years old, buried in Montgomery Co.; Cary, twenty-three, in Frederick Co., and Jesse B., twenty-five, in Anne Arundel Co.

Besides the parents, the family then consisted of three daughters: Bethula, aged thirty-four; Asenath, aged twenty-nine and Mary Ann, aged fourteen and their younger sons, Cary 2nd, aged eleven; Samuel, sixteen, and almost certainly, John aged nineteen years. Whether Asa went with them to Blue Rock, is not clear.

There was a little society of Friends organized at Blue Rock, but whether before or after the arrival of the Hamptons, is not known. True to their inherited ideas of the propriety of both religious and intellectual training of their children, they established a school and Asenath Hampton was the teacher for two summers.

The Doan family, into which Asenath married, had come from Bucks Co., Pennsylvania, in 1820. They had stopped in Jefferson Co., near Mt. Pleasant, for four years and then gone to Muskingum Co., in 1824, settling in

Meigs, an adjoining township to Blue Rock, a few miles from the Hampton home.

The five and a half years at Blue Rock, were eventful ones to the family. Besides the death of James, there were several marriages. Asa married in a little less than two and one-half years after coming to Ohio, and Asenath, about fifteen months later, Samuel twenty months after her, Bethula three months after Samuel and John four and one-half months after Bethula.

Counting Zachariah's, we have six marriages in five years and fifteen days, and five of them in only nine days over three and a half years. Only Mary Ann and Cary 2nd, were left. Only one lived in convenient visiting distance, in those days of toilsome horse-back travel. Asenath was only three miles away, over the county line in Morgan Co. She was also three miles from the Doan home.

James' widow and children and Asa, Bethula and perhaps John were in Belmont Co., in a northeasterly direction over a days journey away, while Zachariah was west of the Muskingum river in Morgan Co., about 18 of 19 miles distant and Samuel two or three miles further in the same county.

In the fall of 1830, the family greatly reduced in size, moved to Belmont Co., and lived near Barnsville, and near "The Ridge" Friends' meeting house. Their grandson, Levi Hamptom, James' second child, writes "Grandfather bought a farm two or three miles from the Ridge in a settlement called "Guinea," on account of the number of colored people living there."

At that time the father was 67 years old, the mother 59, Mary Ann 19 and Cary 16. Their little grandson Levi, was 5 years old. He had gone to live with them after James, his father's death.

About the spring of 1835, (?) they moved to Morgan County, O., near Pennsville and lived in a house built for them on the land owned by their son, Zachariah.

Only the parents with Mary Ann and little grandchild, Levi, composed the family.

In the summer of 1837, on the 14th of 7th month, the wife and mother died. She lacked twelve days of sixty-six years of age, and had lived with her husband fifty years and twenty-four days. She was buried at Pennsville, in the Friends burying ground. Mary Betts Hampton was undoubtedly a good woman. She must have had considerable energy and a spirit of enterprise, for at the time of their removal to Maryland, in 1801, she wanted to go to Ohio, instead, though it was still a part of the northwest territory and hardly cleared of Indians. She appreciated her good blood and breeding and was somewhat aristocratic in her feelings, though not in a bad sense. She was the mother of twelve children, eleven of whom lived to adult years. The average age attained by her children, including the little girl who died at six and one-half years, is over fifty-eight and one-half years. The average age of the whole family, including the parents, is sixty-six years, 10 months, 8 days. The average age of the children who lived to adulthood is sixty-three and one-third years. This is a good average for so large a family.

The subject of the average duration of human life is worthy of the attention of all lovers of their country and race. It tends to confirm the truth of Christianity and to show the value of the science of health. The average duration is generally assumed to be thirty years. Some statistics hardly sustain that view. It has been estimated at 28 and even as low as 26 years. Among the Jews, it is set down at 37. Only the Friends thus far have been proved to have a higher average than the Jews. Tables of mortality, prepared for life insurance companies, among the Friends, some years ago, placed it for them at about 45 1-2 years and for the general public at 40 3-4 years.

But more recent investigations show the average among Friends to be considerably higher, varying from 51 to 58 years, and among the Friends in England, in 1860, it was found to be 59 years. See "Justice to the Jew," by Madison C. Peters.

The statistics, if they were taken, of the larger denominations, and especially of such as are actively evangelistic, gathering in from all classes of society, could not in the very nature of things compare very favorably with the Friends. But if the older families of any of the Protestant churches whose ancestors for several generations, have maintained a generally good Christian character, could be selected by themselves, there can hardly be a doubt that the result would point in the same direction. "Godliness is profitable unto all things having the promise of the life that now is and of that which is to come."

At the death of the wife and mother, the husband soon with the daughter, Mary Ann, moved back to Belmont Co., and lived in a house on his son-in-law, Joseph Arnold's farm, close to the latter's home. Levi who had been a member of the family for about eight years, went to live with his mother, James Hampton's widow who had married his uncle Cary, second.

On the 6th of the 12th month, 1838, Mary Ann married Elihu Robins and her father continued to live with her. Not very long, possibly a little over a year after her marriage, she and her husband moved to Morgan Co., and her father went with them. They lived first in the same house on Zachariah's land where the parent's home had been when the mother died and later on a farm adjoining on the west.

After Mary Ann's marriage, he spent most of the remainder of his life with her, making, however, lengthy visits with his daughter, Asenath, whose home was 25 miles away in Troy township, Athens Co., O., and not far from the village of Coolville. This home was between the Big and Little Hocking rivers about two miles from the former, and four miles from the Ohio river.

He died at the home of his daughter, Mary Ann Robins, on the 3rd day of the 12th month, 1842, in the eightieth year of his age and was buried at Pennsville, in the same buying ground as his wife. He was a teacher at the time of his marriage but whether he continued to teach or if so, how long, is not known. He was also a weaver which in that day of the almost universal wearing of "home spun" clothing, was a very common and useful employment. This business was continued by the family in Maryland in connection with farming.

Though not of very great physicial strength, he was naturally mechanical and used tools well. In the summer of 1840, when well advanced in his seventy-sixth year, he made a "five post hay barrack" for his son-in-law, William Doan. The roof was thatched with straw in the old style of the English and eastern Pennsylvania farmers and was a regular pentagon (five sided) at the base. The rafters made of oak poles came together at a point at their upper ends. The straw was prepared for him out of wheat thrashed with a flail and carefully kept straight as it had been in the sheaf. This he laid on laths made of small saplings split and tied onto the rafters with small withes. The straw was fastened in its place with narrow splints used as strings. The roof was built with the base or eave plates resting on supports near the ground and a tall post, perhaps fifteen feet high, standing in each of the five corners. Holes bored with a large auger about 15 inches apart in the posts with long, strong wood pins, made it easy to raise the roof, a corner at a time, as the space beneath was being filled with hay. Then in winter, as the hay was taken out, the roof was lowered in like manner. This made an excellent substitute for a hay barn which lasted several years.

The same summer, he made baskets from splints from young oak trees. The heavier work was done with an ax and a drawing knife, but the finer finishing, with a large pocket knife.

He had a singular peculiarity in handling tools. Being right-handed, he used tools generally as right-handed men do but a knife he used with his left hand and used it well. He explained this once to my father, by saying that when a boy he and other boys tried the experiment of using their pocket knives with their left hand and he continued it till he could use the knife better with his left hand than with his right.

He had lost his teeth when I remember him best, but I do not remember his ever having any difficulty in eating. Anna Hampton writes that her father told his children that their grandfather could eat anything after he had lost his teeth and that he believed his father's gums were so hard that he could have cracked a hickory nut with them.

He liked fish and greatly enjoyed catching them. I knew him to ride two miles one evening to the Hocking river and back again to set a large hook hoping to catch a large catfish. He rode down to the river again the next morning only to find the bait gone and no fish.

He never seemed happier in his old age than when going fishing with a company of his little grandsons. On one of these occasions, going wearily home after a day's fishing, he told us a story that has been so helpful to me all through life, that I insert it here. It was an Indian story and the event probably occured on or about Penn's purchase of Indian lands. It ran thus:

"An Indian had killed a deer and hung it up on a tree to dress it. Having left it a while to cool, he returned later to take it home but found it was gone. He started out to find his venison, describing the thief as a "little, old, white man who had a short gun." His minute description of the thief whom he had not yet seen, surprised his white friends whom he met and he proceeded to tell how he knew these things. He knew the thief had a short gun because he saw where he had set it down against a tree. The muzzle of the gun had knocked off a piece of bark and the space between the spot on the ground where the gun had rested and the place where the bark was knocked off was so small, he knew the gun was short. He knew the thief was a little man because he had to get a chunk to stand on to get the deer down. He knew that he was a white man because his tracks showed that he turned his toes outward as he walked, whereas an Indian kept his toes straight before him. And he knew he was an old man because he took short steps up hill." This perhaps is not a new story to some of my readers, but if it should help the younger ones as it has helped me to realize the value of observation and reflection it will repay the writing of it. The moral is keep your eyes open as you go and think carefully about what you see. One of my observations has been that there are many people who do not look far ahead nor think down to the roots of things.

Like the Friends generally, our grandfather Hampton, favored all moral reforms. At that day two topics of this nature were prominently before the people, intemperance and slavery. He was opposed to both.

Talking thoughtfully, one Sabbath afternoon, on the question of slavery, he expressed the "fear that it would yet go down in an ocean of blood." This was twenty or twenty-one years before the beginning of the civil war, and when those dreadful days were passing by I used to think, sometimes, of grandfather's fears, expressed so long before.

Their son, John, bears this testimony in regard to the religious lives of his parents, John and Mary Betts Hampton: "They adhered strictly to Friend's principles and testimonies and from expressions of their peace and lively hope of a happy eternity, gave to survivors, the very comfortable hope that their end was peace and that they are eternally at rest."

Lineage of the Children of John and Mary Betts Hampton as far as it has been ascertained at this writing, February 7th, 1906.

1. CARY
2. JESSE B.
3. BETHULA
4. JAMES
5. ASENATH
6. ZACHARIAH
7. ASA
8. SARAH
9. JOHN
10. SAMUEL
11. MARGAM
12. CARY, 2nd.

JOHN HAMPTON
Born 1763-10-16

- JOHN HAMPTON
  Born 1724-1-12
  - JOSEPH HAMPTON, of England { E. S. Beckman, Philadelphia, says Scotland
  - Made declaration of marriage 1722-8-9 with
  - MARY CANBY
    Born 1697-9-12
    - THOMAS CANBY. born in England, 1667
    - Married 1693-9-2
    - SARAH JARVIS, of Abington.
- M
- ANN CROSSDALE
  Born 1730-11-15
  - JEREMIAH CROSSDALE
    Born 1694-8-29
    - EZRA CROSSDALE, of England
    - Married 1687-2-6
    - ANN PEACOCK, of England
  - Married
  - GRACE HEATON

M. 1787-6-20

MARY BETTS
Born 1771-7-26

- ZAZHARIAH BETTS
  - THOMAS BETTS, of Long Island
  - Married
  - SUSANNA FIELD, in New Jersey
    Born 1703 or 4, died 1788-3—?
- M
- BETHULA CARY
  - SAMUEL CARY, gentleman of England
  - Married
  - SARAH STACKHOUSE, said to have been "an eminent Minister among the Friends."

*EXPLANATION—The Friends required a declaration of intention to marry in one session of a monthly meeting and continuation of intention in the next session, then the marriage at the next week day meeting, so that this marriage must have been over a month later or about the last of September, 1722.

Fourth Generation

17 CARY (4) HAMPTON, (John 3, John 2, Joseph 1) born the 4th of the 5th month, 1788, in Bucks Co., Penn., died the 21st of the 8th month, 1911. Unmarried. He was Buried in Bush Creek Friend's burying ground, Frederick Co., Maryland.

18 JESSE B. (4) HAMPTON, (John 3, John 2, Joseph 1) born the 21st of the 7th month 1789 in Bucks Co., Penn. Married ARAMINTA FISHER, daughter of John and Araminta Fisher, 5th of the 5th month, 1814. He was a carpenter. His wife was a good, pious young woman and a member of the Methodist church. He died the 14th of the 1st month, 1815, and was buried in his wife's family burying ground in Anne Arundel Co., Maryland. They had one child, Jesse, born after his father's death.

19 BETHULA (4) HAMPTON, (John 3, John 2, Joseph 1) born 1st of the 8th month, 1791. Married on the 21st of the 12th month, 1829, in Blue Rock Township, Muskingum Co., Ohio, where her father then lived, to Joseph Arnold, of near Barnsville, Belmont Co., Ohio. After the death of her husband she married Anderson Arnold, a cousin of her first husband. She died the 4th of the 12th month, 1855. Always a member of the society of Friends, and after her marriage held her membership at the Ridge meeting near Barnsville. She furnished a home for a while for her father and for her younger sister Mary Ann. No children.

20 JAMES (4) HAMPTON, (John 3, John 2, Joseph 1) born the 26th of the 6th month, 1794, at Wrightstown, Bucks Co., Penn. Married on the 4th of the 10th month,

1820, EMILY WALTON, daughter of Amos and Elizabeth Walton, of Lancaster Co., Penn. He was a weaver and a school teacher and taught both in Pennsylvania and Ohio His son James Hiram writes:: "I remember a beautiful bedspread which my mother had and which she told me my father wove. My father was a fine penman. I have seen some of his ornamental writing that was exceedingly fine. He moved to Ohio with his father's family about the 1st of May, 1825, and settled in Belmont Co. He taught for several years, but his teaching became interrupted by poor health and he finally died the 24th of the 6th month, 1829, aged 35 years.

His youngest son has furnished a note which throws light on the cause of his father's death, as follows: "I have often heard my mother say that father's death resulted from the effect of an internal injury received several years before while handling a vicious cow and that he was never stout after he was hurt. That the immediate cause of his last sickness was a severe cold, contracted while sitting near an open window acting as clerk of the Ohio Yearly Meeting of Friends. I am of the opinion that it was pulmonary abscess rather than consumption."

(Signed) James Hiram Hampton.

Children:

29 I AMOS W., born the 12th of the 11th month, 1822.

30 II LEVI, born the 17th of the 3rd month, 1825.

31 III MARY, born the 3rd of the 1st month, 1827.

32 IV JAMES HIRAM, born the 21st of the 2nd month, 1829, and died the 19th of the 11th month, 1910.

21

ASENATH (4) HAMPTON, (John 3, John 2, Joseph 1) born at Wrightstown Township, Bucks Co., Penn., on the 3rd day of the 3rd month, 1796. In 1801 was moved with her parents to Maryland and in 1825 to Ohio. Before leaving Maryland she had assisted her brother, Zachariah, in teaching a school in Loudon Co., Va. After going to Ohio she assisted her brother, James, in teaching in Belmont Co., at or near Flushing. She taught two summers in Blue Rock township, Muskingum Co. She married William Doan, son of Daniel and Mary Plumly Doan, on the 24th of the 1st month, 1828. He was of the seventh generation of American Doanes and decended from Deacon John Doane, of Plymouth colony. He was born in Philadelphia Co., Penn., 1799-4-20. Learned the coachmakers trade in Bucks Co., where his youth was mostly spent. Came to Ohio in 1820. Worked some at ironing wagons and at other blacksmithing in Ohio, but spent most of his life on a farm. Was very neat and mechanical in all his work. Was especially interested in the cultivation of fruit, and had the finest collection of apples and other fruits in the community where he lived. He was greatly interested in public affairs, especially such as involved a moral quality. Never scrambling for office, he became a leader of public opinion in his neighborhood whose motives could not be impugned. After Asenath's marriage she and her husband settled in Bristol Township, Morgan Co., about three miles from her father's and about the same distance from his father's. Here her children were born, as follows:

I JOHN HAMPTON DOAN, born the 10th of the 12th month, 1828.

II MARY DOAN, born the 3rd of the 9th month, 1830.

III JAMES DOAN, born the 22nd of the 2nd month, 1832.

IV ANN HAMPTON DOAN, born the 12th of the 2nd month, 1834.

Moved on New Years day, 1836, to Meigs Township, Muskingum Co., near the Doan homestead and also near Lytlesburg, about four miles from the Bristol home. Moved again in the fall of the same year to Chesterfield, (Athens) now Morgan Co., Ohio. Finally moved—15th of the 5th month, 1839 to Troy township, Athens Co., near Coolvile, Ohio. Here was her home the remainder of her life. She died the 4th of the 12th month, 1885, and was buried beside her husband in the Friend's old burying ground in Decatur Township in Washington Co., Ohio.

She was a lover of learning and greatly admired good poetry. In her younger days, when books were scarce, she copied many pieces of poetry. Had also a love of flowers and shrubbery and cultivated them with taste. She guided her household affairs with discretion and governed her family well. She sometimes took part in business meetings of her church, but was more active in anti-slavery and temperance meetings. Living so long in her early life in a slave state, she saw much in the condition of the slaves which pained her keen sense of right and wrong. As early as 1838 she cheerfully concented to the opening of her house for the first anti-slavery lecturer that appeared when a public building could not be obtained. Her natural hatred of all things vile caused her to despise the traffic in intoxicating liquors and to take an abiding interest in the temperance cause. She was often called on to speak in the meetings of the temperance society which was organized near her home in 1842 and maintained for about ten years. Some of her opinions on religious subjects were not strictly orthodox, but her morality was orthodox. Perhaps her most striking characteristic was an intense desire to do right and to spread the reign of righteousness. In her last illness she was frequently delirious and at such times often praying vocally and the burden of her prayers was, "I want to do right. Lord teach me what is right." This thought was in harmony with her life. For further notice of Asenath Doan and husband, see Asenath Hampton Gable, No. 59.

22 ZACHARIAH BETTS (4) HAMPTON, (John 3, John 2, Joseph 1) born the 25th of the 1st month, 1798, at Wrightstown, (or possibly Middletown) Township, Bucks Co., Penn. Was moved with the family to Maryland in 1801.

There is no record of his early school days known to the writer but later he attended the Brandywine Friends Boarding School. He taught school in Loudon Co., Virginia, and perhaps, also in Maryland, before coming to

Ohio. He came to Ohio in advance of the family, in the year of 1824. Attended the Ohio Yearly Meeting (at Mt. Pleasant, probably) in the fall of that year. He "took up" 80 acres of land near Pennsville, Morgan Co., and located a home for his parents in Blue Rock township, Muskingum Co. He taught school at Flushing, Belmont Co., and on the 20th of the 4th month, 1825, married SARAH GRIFFITH, at Red Stone Friend's Meeting House, near Cookstown, Pennsylvania. This church was a branch of the Ohio Yearly Meeting.

The land he had purchased in Morgan Co., "was all in the woods and heavily timbered." Here in the fall of 1825 he reared a log cabin into which they moved. Here their children were born as follows:

33 I WILLIAM, born the 14th of the 3rd month, 1826.

34 II RUTH COPE, born the 2nd of the 1st month, 1828.

III LYDIA, born the 14th of the 8th month, 1830, died the 7th of the 6th month, 1845.

35 IV SARAH GRIFFITH, born the 18th of the 5th month, 1832.

36 V MARY ELMA, born the 8th of the 2nd month, 1835.

His principal occupation, afterward, was farming, including fruit culture.

"He studied surveying and did a little at that in the opening of the farms there in Ohio," his daughter, Sarah, says, and adds "he studied medicine but did not practice much except in his family, but went some as nurse." He remained on the farm near Pennsville, till the fall of 1851, when he moved his family to Iowa and settled near Viola, Linn Co., going overland in a "prairie schooner" and a buggy and they were just four weeks on the way. It was in October.

He died 18th of the 4th month, 1861. He was a zealous member of the orthodox society of Friends and active in the affairs of the church. He served as clerk of the meeting at Pennsville.

He was a lover and a cultivator of fruit and had a large collection of fine varieties of apples on his farm in Ohio, in a few years after it was opened up. Had a small nursery in the later years of his stay in Ohio and became a member of the county Horticultural Society. On one occasion he was appointed as a committee to name an apple which had not a satisfactory name. Was once a delegate to the State Horticultural convention at Columbus. He was a lover and a promoter of learning. In the winter of 1843, he with others, organized a "Phylosophy School," which held weekly evening meetings in the Friends' school house, between his home and Pennsville, for the study of natural phylosophy, or physics, as now more generally called. A Dr. Vail, of Pennsville, was a helper and likely a member of the organization. It was my privilege to be present one evening when the doctor was there with his electricial machine. It was the first I had ever seen and the lesson learned and the benefit derived, remain to this day. The text book used was Comstock's Natural Phylosophy.

I was frequently at Uncle Zachariah's house that winter and seized every convenient opportunity to read that book. It was an inspiration and an uplift to me. My visits to his home were always pleasant and profitable to me and their memory is vivid to this day.

Like other Friends, he was opposed to slavery and aided runaway slaves when he could. His daughter says his home "was a stopping place on the underground railroad."

Politically, in his early life, he was a Whig. Later, he sympathized with the Republican party but never voted after its organization, his daughter Sarah, says.

SARAH GRIFFITH, wife of Zachariah Hampton, was born the 2nd of the 8th month, 1803, in Fayette Co., Pennsylvania, near Cookstown. She was the daughter of William and Sarah (Cook) Griffith and a descendant in the sixth generation on her mother's side, of Peter Cook, of Tarvin, Cheshire, England, and Elinor Norman, of Kingley, Cheshire, England, who were married at Newton, in Cheshire, December 7th, 1695.

Sarah (Griffith) Hampton, lived after her husband's death, over twenty-five years, and died 9th month, 22nd,

1886. She was also a zealous Friend. Both were buried at Hopewell church, near Viola, Ia.

23 ASA C. (4) HAMPTON, (John 3, John 2, Joseph 1) born 5th month, 7th, 1800, in Bucks Co., Penn. In 1801, was moved with his parents, to Maryland, and lived there with the family, as related in their history, till 1825. Then moved with them to Ohio. It is not certain whether he lived with the family at Blue Rock. He did live several years in Barnsville. His son, James, says he taught school several years in Barnsville, Belmont Co. Married ESTHER PATTERSON 10th of the 10th month, 1827, a native of North Carolina. She had two brothers, Laban, a "Thomsonian" doctor, who lived in Ohio, and later in Linn Co., Ia., and Lemuel, who lived in Belmont Co., O.

Children:

37 I MARTHA, born the 10th month, 8th, 1828.

II JOSEPH, born 2nd month, 11th, 1830. "An ingenious, bright boy," but was short lived, dying in Mt. Vernon, Iowa, 11th month, 19th, 1850.

38 III BENJAMIN FRANKLIN, born 11th month, 22nd, 1831.

39 IV ELI GRIFFITH, born 5th month, 10th, 1833.

40 V JAMES W., born 1st month, 24th, 1835.

VI RUTH, born 12th month, 19th, 1836. Her case was singular. In the first winter of her life, she had whooping cough in a malignant form. At one time was thought to be dying, if not already dead. But she rallied and till about two years old, her father thought her one of the brightest, if not the brightest child he had. But she became enfeebled mentally and was a great care. She died 4th month, 20th, 1852, in her sixteenth year.

VII PHEBE, born 2nd month, 20th, 1839. "At the age of six years, she had scarlet fever, which left her with a very serious nervous affection, from which she never recovered It effected her both physically and mentally, causing her to become a great charge during her entire life afterwards.

She died 12th month, 26th, 1905, and was buried at Palāsade, Colorado, where she died."

41 VIII JESSE, born 9th month, 19th, 1843.

42 IX BETHULA ANN, born 4th month, 30th, 1846.

Asa Hampton, the father of this family, probably learned shoe-making, as well as farming, in Maryland, and likely practiced it in Belmont Co., for after going to Chesterfield, it was his employment for a while. Chesterfield was then in Athens, but since in Morgan Co. Whether he went directly from Belmont to Chesterfield or whether he first went to Pennsville, Morgan Co., for a few years, is not quite clear. His son, James W., thinks or has thought through life, that he was born at Pennsville. His birth occured in January, 1835, and if it was at Pennsville, the family must have gone to Chesterfield soon after, for in October, 1836, they were living in a house, apparently at least, several months old which he had built in Chesterfield. Pennsville is six miles nearer Belmont, on the then commonly traveled road to the latter.

About the summer of 1837, he entered into partnership with a potter, named Jonathan Naylor, and engaged in the manufacture of what was then known as earthen ware. This was not long continued, probably because the clay in the neighborhood, was not well adapted to the purpose.

About the end of 1838, or early in 1839, he sold his home in Chesterfield, and purchased a farm near (about two miles north of) Plymouth, Washington Co., and about six miles eastward of Chesterfield. Here he remained till about the spring, probably, of 1845, when, because of the financial condition of the country in those days, he was compelled to sell his farm, not being able to complete the payment of the purchase price.

He rented in two places between Plymouth and Chesterfield. Then in 1847, he bought 40 acres of heavily timbered land for $200 in the edge of Athens Co., but not far from Plymouth and in a southwesterly direction. It was to be paid for in tobacco at $4.00 per hundred weight.

He built a double log house on it and cleared about 20 acres of the land which he planted, mostly, in tobacco. Had a good crop and paid for his land. In the spring of 1850, he sold the land for $400, and moved into Plymouth, where he remained about two months. In all these places where he lived near and in Plymouth, he did shoemaking, his growing boys being more and more able to do the farm work year after year.

"When he sold the little farm in Athens Co., he had to take the pay in a blind horse, at $50.00, and in personal notes for the rest. The notes he traded to a tanner named Harmon Rhodes, near Plymouth, for shoe leather, which he took to Iowa with him and manufactured into boots and shoes."

"He started for Iowa about the 5th of the 5th month, 1850, with two teams going overland and taking his family, consisting of a wife and nine children, and making the journey in 27 days. At that time there were but seven miles of railroad in the state of Iowa. They arrived at Cedar Rapids, then a town of 15 or 20 houses, built mostly of sod or slabs, 6th month, 1st, 1850."

"He then dropped back after a few days to Mt. Vernon, Linn Co. Opening a shoe shop there, he engaged in the business for two years, when he entered government land near what is now called Viola, also in Linn Co."

He died of typhoid fever, 3rd month, 21st, 1854, and was buried at Viola Friends church. He was an industrious, laborious, energetic man, patient in his family and kind to all. His toilsome life excited my sympathy and the thought of it in connection with his early death, has been a painful one to me for more than fifty years.

His wife, ESTHER PATTERSON HAMPTON, was a mild tempered, kindhearted woman. Some time after her husband died, she left the farm and lived with her daughter, Martha, in Blackhawk Co., where she died the 22nd of the 3rd month, 1857, three years and one day after her husband and was buried at Poyner's graveyard.

24 JOHN (4) HAMPTON, (John 3, John 2, Joseph 1) was born at Sandy Spring, Montgomery Co., Md., the 26th of the 2nd month, 1806, moved with the family to Frederick Co., Md., in 1808. Moved again with the family in the spring of 1825, to Ohio, where he probably at first lived for a time with his parents, at Blue Rock township, Muskingum Co. Later he taught school in Belmont Co. The 5th of the 5th month, 1830, he married MARY WILLIAMS, at or near Somerton, O., in the bounds of Somerton Monthly Meeting of Friends.

She was the daughter of Samuel and Sarah (Arnold) Williams and was born the 4th month 28th, 1812, between Bridgeport and Mt. Pleasant, O., her daughter thinks.

Anna writes "Our mother was a good woman. Did her part in her household as near as anyone could. Was a good housekeeper and a good cook and if there was a good woman anywhere, I think she was one." She was a worker in our society, The Society of Friends. It appears that he moved to Pennsville, Morgan Co., not long after marriage, for his daughter, Sarah, whose birth occured 12th month, 2nd, 1832, says she was born there.

About 1835, it is thought, he assisted his brother-in-law, Axum or Exum Bundy, in laying out the town of Chesterfield, then in Athens Co., but since transfered to Morgan Co.

In this new town he built a house which he lived in till the spring of 1839. He followed carpentering here as likely he had elsewhere. He returned to Belmont Co., in the spring of 1839, and continued to do carpenter work, living in several places and finally "bought a saw mill near Barnsville and lived there for several years."

In 1854, the family moved to Linn Co., Iowa. They went overland in two carriages and a wagon. Started 4th month, 5th, and arrived 5th month, 10th. Settled at Viola, where he purchased 80 acres of land of his brother Samuel. He added more to it afterward. On arrival he built a log cabin immediately in which they lived two years when his son Oliver and a cousin built him "quite a good house," in which he and his wife spent the remainder of their lives.

He was a farmer ever after going to Iowa, until he became unable to work, when at about eighty-four years old, he sold his farm to his grandson, Samuel Mott, but continued to live in a part of the house.

Children:

43 I OLIVER L., born 2nd of the 3rd month, 1831.
44 II SARAH W., born 2nd of the 12th month, 1832.
45 III ROBERT, born the 13th of the 6th month, 1835.
46 IV LUCINDA, born the 23rd of the 6th month, 1837.
47 V ANNA, born the 3rd of the 4th month, 1840.
48 VI ELIZA, born the 5th of the 4th month, 1844.
49 VII LOVINA, born the 27th of the 6th month, 1846.
VIII JOHN, born in 1849, and died in 1850, near one year old.
50 IX EDWARD, born 2nd of the 7th month, 1851.
X SAMUEL, twin to Edward, lived near two months.

He had good control of his family and governed without severity. When a boy I admired his family government. He was a member of the orthodox Friends and was an active worker in the church. He was an overseer and a clerk in the meetings of his society for several years. "Was strictly orthodox and a full believer in a Savior. He was a real peace man." Thus his daughter writes of him and adds: "I might say he was a very good man in his family." "He was a great lover of poetry and had many poems written down."

He was opposed to slavery and became a member of the first anti-slavery society organized in the community where he lived. This was in Chesterfield, in the winter of 1838. He never used intoxicating liquors as a beverage nor tobacco. Was temperate, industrious and steady going in his habits. Was in sympathy with the "Free-soil" and Republican parties in their antagonism to the extension of slavery but never an active politician.

He was much attached to his kindred and relatives

and some years after going to Iowa, projected a plan for keeping up a correspondence among them by means of a budget of circular letters called "The Little Traveler," which has been continued since his death to this writing, June, 1907. This budget of letters traveling around among a dozen or fifteen families of the Hamptons and their relatives scattered about in several states, has kept them somewhat in touch with each other, and helped those who have written for it to retain some knowledge of the whereabouts of even some who did not write in it. Largely, by means of this "Little Traveler," the notion of preparing this history was developed and found to be feasible.

He died 4th month, 19, 1898.

25

SAMUEL BETTS (4) HAMPTON, (John 3, John 2, Joseph 1) was born in Frederick Co., Maryland, on the 9th of the 4th month, 1809. In the spring of 1825, when about one month passed sixteen years of age, he moved with his father's family, to Ohio, and settled on a farm at Blue Rock, Muskingum Co.

On the 23rd of the 9th month, 1829, he married ELIZABETH PIERPOINT, daughter of Jonathan and Ann Pierpoint, of Morgan Co., Ohio. The Pierpoint home was on Wolf Creek, a few miles south of Pennsville. They owned a flour and saw mill on Wolf Creek and Jonathan Pierpoint followed milling for many years.

They evidently came from Columbiana Co., Ohio, to Wolf Creek, but whence the husband came from to Columbiana Co., does not appear. His wife, whose maiden name was Ann Steer, was born in Loudon Co., Virginia. Her people, who remained in Loudon Co., were a good family, reported to have been in good circumstances before the civil war, but their home being near "the border," was plundered by both armies and they were left in destitute circumstances. They were Unionists.

Just where Samuel Hampton and his bride first made their home and what was his occupation at first, is not now known, but the home was no doubt near the Pierpoint mill, and the occupation farming or carpentry or both combined.

About five or six years later, he moved into the newly laidout village of Chesterfield, four or five miles away over the county line and then in Athens Co., where his occupation was carpentering and cabinetmaking. After a few years he built a brick house in the south end of the town which he occupied both as a home for his family and as a public house for the entertainment of travelers. After ten or more years in Chesterfield, in the spring of 1846, he moved back to the Pierpoint neighborhood and lived on a farm three miles south of Pennsville. Here he remained five years when in the fall of 1851, the family moved to Iowa, going overland in wagons. They were 21 days on the way. He purchased land near Viola, Linn Co., about 17 miles distant from Cedar Rapids, and engaged in farming. His daughter, Mary, writes: "He was naturally mechanical and very ingenious with tools—could manufacture a fine piece of mahogany furniture and as readily build a house or a barn."

She also refers to his being like his father in his love for fish and of fishing and says: "Times without number, do I remember his getting a few neighbors and fishing materials together and taking two horses and a wagon for an all night work in the Muskingum river near McConnelsville. They usually came back with a good supply of nice large fishes which my father could not enjoy till his neighbors were supplied." Twice, also, while he lived in Chesterfield, he made a trip to the home of his sister, 20 miles away to fish, once in the Big Hocking river and once in the Little Hocking.

Of his anti-slavery opinions and practices, she writes: "Having lived in a slave state and witnessed much cruelty in the treatment of the slaves, he became greatly interested in their behalf and early espoused their cause. He was ever ready to assist them in obtaining their freedom. At one time he with a few of his friends, secretly fed a company of sixteen in a cave four miles from Chesterfield, Ohio. The slave owners were on their track and the usually quiet village was in a great state of excitement which, however, soon passed off as the hunters grew weary and left the place. It was now considered safe to proceed and the little band who were loyal to the slaves, sixteen in number, under cover of the night, escorted the fugitives to the next "underground station." There was $1600 offered for the capture of the slaves."

"Later, while living in Iowa, when the poor unfortunates found their way to his door, they were taken in a covered wagon as though going to market, at Dubuque, and from there forwarded to Canada. Of his moral and religious character, she writes: "He was a member of the orthodox branch of the Friends church, strictly moral and upright, although he did not experience a change of heart until he was 65 years of age. Would speak of it with great regret that he had lived so long without a religious experience. The change wrought a wonderful transformation. Always manifesting a meek and quiet spirit, now he became even more tender and Christ-like in his life, striving to better the condition of those about him and gathering in the children to teach them the scriptures. He died at the home of his son, Richard, in Davis Co., Kansas, of neuralgia of the heart, 11th month, 17th, 1883."

His wife, Elizabeth Pierpoint Hampton, "was a woman of a quiet temperament, ever ready to help the poor and unfortunate. Owing to poor health she seldom went from home. She was a warm friend of the slaves, and all that were oppressed, a real mother and a home maker." She outlived her husband a little more than a year and died 1st month, 20th, 1885.

Children:

1 ANN born 7th month, 11th, 1830, died 2nd month, 28th, 1833.

51 II JONATHAN, born the 5th month, 30th, 1832.

52 III MARY, born the 10th month, 15th, 1836.

53 IV ANN PIERPOINT, born 11th month, 5th, 1838.

54 V ISAAC STEER, born 2nd month, 8th, 1841.

55 VI RICHARD BETTS, born 2nd month, 21st, 1844.

56 VII WILLIAM STEER, born 2nd month, 8th, 1847.

VIII ASA, born 5th month, 14th, 1856, died March 17th, 1880. He had married Ruth ————. No children.

26 MARY ANN (4) HAMPTON, (John 3, John 2, Joseph) was born 1811-2-1, in Frederick Co., Md. In 1825, moved with her parents to Ohio and lived in several places with them as related in their history. On December 6th, 1838, she was married to ELIHU ROBINS, in the Friends church at the "Ridge" near Barnsville, Belmont Co., O. They lived first on the farm of Joseph Arnold, husband of her older sister, Bethula, in Belmont, but moved ere long to Morgan Co., and lived on the farm of her brother, Zachariah, and later rented an adjoining farm a mile or more south of Pennsville.

In the spring of 1846, they moved to Iowa, going by the way of the Ohio and Mississippi rivers on steam boats.

They first lived at or near Salem, Henry Co. Had charge of a saw mill about four miles from Salem on Cedar Creek and engaged in lumber business.

In February, 1850, moved to Cedar Rapids, Linn Co., Ia., which was the family home ever after, except that the husband sought fortune in the Colorado mines in 1860, but like so many others, found it not. Previous to going to the mines, he had been a contractor and builder and a manufacturer of lime. Added packing and delivering of ice to his business.

After returning from the mines he bought a farm joining the city limits and engaged in gardening and raising small fruits. On September 27th, 1888, their home, a good, well furnished and nearly new house, was burned. "The family just escaped with their lives and got a few things out of the house." A heavy stroke truly. The wife 78 years old and the husband 80, but they had friends and fortunately an insurance of $1000 on the house and $500 on the furniture and were enabled to rebuild.

A little more than two months later on Dec. 6th, 1888, a company of their friends in Cedar Rapids, gathered at the home of their son, Oliver, and sent for them. It was a party in honor of the fiftieth anniversary of their marriage and a complete surprise. The gifts were many and valuable and well adapted to the condition of the family so soon after the fire.

She adhered to the orthodox Friends in whose fellowship she had been raised till after going to Iowa.

She had a natural gift for drawing and painting which to me, in my boyhood, seemed remarkable. She had to make her own paints and brushes of such materials as she could command. Her paintings were of flowers and birds only, I think, but impressed me as being so natural and good as to cause me many times in later years to regret that she could not have had the privilege of instruction by an artist.

She died Nov. 3rd, 1902, aged over 91 3-4 years.

Elihu Robins, her husband, was born in Belmont Co., O., in July, 1808, was raised in an adjoining county, (Guernsey it is thought). Like his wife, he belonged to the orthodox Friends in Ohio. He early espoused the Anti-slavery cause and on one occasion, at least, helped to aid runaway slaves to escape.

This was in 1843. In 1844 he voted the Liberty party ticket. When the Republican party was organized, as most Anti-slavery men did, he went into it and was an ardent Republican the remainder of his life.

Children of Mary Ann (Hampton) Robins:

I ZACHARIAH HAMPTON, (Robins) born 1839-12-11.

II WILLIAM DOAN, (Robins) born 1842-4-3.

III CLARA ASENATH, (Robins) born 1843-11-23, died 1880-4-23.

IV ANNA E., (Robins) born 1846-10-9.

V OLIVER W., (Robins) born 1850-7-14.

VI ASA HAMPTON, (Robins) born 1853-2-26.

First three in Ohio and the other three in Iowa.

27 CARY (4) HAMPTON, (John 3, John 2, Joseph 1) born 7th month, 17th, 1814, in Frederick Co., Md. His oldest brother who was also named Cary, having been then dead nearly three years, the name was given to him.

In the spring of 1825, he moved with his father's family to Blue Rock Tp., Muskingum Co., Ohio, and in the fall of 1830, to Belmont Co. He also lived awhile with his older brother, Zachariah, near Pennsville, Morgan Co.

Some time in 1835, he married EMILY (WALTON) HAMPTON, his brother James' widow, at her home on the farm of Lemuel Patterson, near Barnsville, Belmont Co., Ohio. The ceremony was performed by a justice of the peace. This being a violation of the law of the Friends church, they lost their membership therein.

Soon after marriage they moved some miles further west into Guernsey Co., and lived on the farm of a Mr. Solomon Eagin or Egan, and later at another place not far away.

About this time a great change came over their religious opinions. They became associated with the denomination called Disciples but popularly known as Campbellites, which title, however, they disclaimed. In 1838, or early in 1839, they moved to a place on the Ohio river in Washington Co., about five or six miles below Marietta.

In the spring of 1840, they moved over to the Virginia side and located a little higher up the river just above the foot of Muskingum Island, and about five miles below Marietta at a place called Cole's Wood Yard, where he engaged in supplying cord wood for the steamboats.

Here their youngest child, Asenath, was born.

In the early spring of 1841, he placed their goods and family on a small flatboat and floated down about 15 miles, to the mouth of the Little Hocking river, whence they were hauled out about four miles to the place of William Doan, his sister Asenath's husband, where he had already built a cabin and taken a lease of timber land to be cleared.

This was in Athens Co., O. Here he remained two years, supporting himself and family with some help from his stepsons, by doing labor of different kinds but largelly by "turning" wooden bowls at which he was an expert.

It was here, probably, that he first exercised his gifts as a preacher. There was a little church of the disciples about a mile away and he was a very active member. He also began to visit other places.

In the spring of 1843, they moved a few miles away over the county line, into Washington Co., again, and in Belpre Tp., near the mouth of the Little Hocking river. Lived later in Decatur and still later, near Plymouth, both in the same county.

In the latter place he taught school and preached for the Disciples. "In 1846, or early in 1847, he moved to Meigs Co., and lived near Pomeroy. Here he practiced medicine having been studying for some time and having practiced a little, Hiram thinks while living near Plymouth.

On February 7th, 1850, his wife, Emily (Walton) Hampton, died. As before related, she had been the wife of his older brother, James, and mother of James' four children: Amos W., Levi, Mary and James Hiram. She was born 1798-10-24, in a Friends or Quaker family, in Penn., and continued to be a member of the society during the life of her first husband and through her widowhood.

Hiram writes: "I will say that my mother, during many of the later years of her life, was an earnest Christian and died in the triumphs of faith. I was not with her when she died. Did not know she was sick till after she was buried, but her dying message to me was: 'Tell Hiram I believe his father is in Heaven and I know that I am going and I want to meet him there.' Said 'Dying is hard, but O, the peace. Glory to God, I am going home to Heaven.'"

Solomon speaks of her life as an inspiration to others.

Children of Cary and Emily:

57 I EMILY, born 1836-4-30, in Guernsey Co., Ohio.

58 II SOLOMON ERNEST, born 1837-9-14.

59 III ASENATH, born 1840-7-2, in Wood Co., Va., now West Virginia.

After Emily's death, Cary "went to Bethany, Va., where he was a frequent visitor at the home of that noted character, Alexander Campbell, of whom he was a great admirer."

While at Bethany "he married in 1851, SARAH DAVIS, a noble Christian woman," his son Solomon, says, "and soon after located in Pike Co., O., and resumed the practice of medicine at a little town called California, and did well for a few years and then moved to Buckhanon Co., Iowa, where his wife died.

By his second wife he had one child:
MOHALA MELVINA, born ————, in Ohio.

He died at Mansfield, O., 1889-3-18. He was a ready and fluent speaker and labored strenously to propagate the new doctrine he had espoused. Enjoyed debating on the subject and lectured much on temperance.

Asenath thought he voted the Prohibition ticket in later years.

Fifth Generation

28

JESSE B. (5) HAMPTON, (Jesse Betts 4, John 3, John 2, Joseph 1) was born in Anne Arundel Co., Feb. 20th, 1815, twenty-nine days after his father's death for whom he was named. In the year 1829, when in his fifteenth year, he came with his mother to Ohio to visit his father's people and spent part of the summer with them.

My mother's record says he married and settled in Anne Arundel, Co., but late in life she told me that he had been living in Baltimore and that the last report was that he had died and left no children.

29

AMOS WALTON (5) HAMPTON, (James 4, John 3, John 2, Joseph 1) was born 11th month, 12th, 1822, in Pennsylvania. Was taken by his parents to Belmont Co., O., in 1825. By death, left without a father's care in 1829, lived with his mother till after her second marriage. Leaving her he went first to live with his uncle and aunt, Joseph and Bethula Arnold, near Barnsville, O. In 1843, he went to work on the farm of Jonathan Bundy, at or near "The Ridge."

He married 1844-2-8, Jonathan's daughter, MARY BUNDY. They lived on her father's place a year and then went to a place called Stillwater, for a few years.

While living at "The Ridge," he taught school.

Amos and wife moved to Iowa in the spring of 1850, going by water to Keokuk. Thence to Salem, Henry Co., in wagons, where he engaged in farming till the spring of 1854, when they moved to West Branch, Cedar Co., where they remained till after the civil war. They sold out and went to Missouri to teach the freed men. "It was too soon after the war. The southern element was too strong. So they went into the edge of Kansas, Cherokee Co., and bought land," where he engaged in farming and gardening "and took produce to the miners at Joplin, Mo."

Here in Cherokee Co., he was approved as a minister among the Friends and engaged in work in behalf of the ex-slaves or freedmen. He was troubled with asthma and in 1883, went to Wilsey, a small place in Morris Co., and engaged in the grocery business. But his health did not improve. Here he died, 1887-6-16.

Mary Bundy Hampton, his wife, soon after his death, went to live with her sister and brother-in-law, Lydia and Jonathan Hampton.

30

LEVI (5) HAMPTON, (James 4, John 3, John 2, Joseph 1) was born 1825-3-17, in Pennsylvania. Brought by his parents to Belmont Co., O., when a few weeks old. After the death of his father in his fifth year, he was taken to live with his grandfather and grandmother Hampton, at Blue Rock, Muskingum Co., and continued to live with them as related in their history till the death of his grandmother in 1837, when he was a little over 12 years old, after which he went to live with his mother and her husband, his uncle Cary Hampton, in Guernsey Co. A little later he went to live with his aunt, Bethula Arnold, and her husband, near Barnsville, Belmont Co., and as he says, "to hoe his own row in the world."

In the fall of 1840, he went to visit his mother and her family in Wood Co., Va., now West Virginia, and stayed with them there and in Athens Co., O., a year, going back to Belmont in the fall of 1841. He worked at times for his uncle and aunt, Arnold, and stayed with them several winters and went to school.

In 1848 or 1849, he married LYDIA ANN PATTERSON, moved to Salem, Henry Co., Iowa., in 1850. Lost his wife a few weeks after going there in the 3rd month, 1850.

"Worked about for a few years." Then married MARY HACKET, he thinks, about the 9th month, 1855. About the year 1860, they moved to Hardin Co., Iowa, where they continued to live till the wife's death, 1895-11-

28. Was still living in 1905, "a lonely life near the farm on which they first settled in that county."

Friend. Republican. Has held office of overseer in Friends church.

31 MARY (5) HAMPTON, (James 4, John 3, John 2, Joseph 1) was born in Ohio, probably in Belmont Co., 1827-1-3.

Her father died when she was hardly two and one-half years old and she, with two of her brothers, one older and one younger, was left in the care of the mother, who after about six years of widowhood, was married to her husband's youngest brother, Cary. With them she continued to live at various places as related in their history, until about nineteen and one-half years of age, when with their consent, in 1846, probably, she left them at their home near Plymouth, Washington Co., and went to Belmont Co., and had her home with her brother, Amos, for one winter and part of the next summer. She returned to Washington Co., and had her home with her uncle, Asa Hampton, between Plymouth and Chesterfield. Here she was married Sept. 3rd, 1847, to DANIEL GEORGE ELLIS. They lived in Plymouth till May, 1850, when they moved to Linn Co., Iowa, but in the fall of that year, settled in Blackhawk Co., where her home was the remainder of her life. She died 1896-9-20.

She was a member of the Methodist Episcopal church. They furnished a home for a while for her younger half-sister, Asenath. Her husband writes: "Mary Hampton Ellis was a devout Christian and a noble woman loved by everybody." No children.

32 JAMES HIRAM (5) HAMPTON, (James 4, John 3, John 2, Joseph 1) was born 1829-2-21, in Belmont Co., O. When he was about four months old, his father died. When about six years old, his mother married her husband's youngest brother, Cary, and he lived with the family in various places as related in their history till in

his eighteenth year, being a very helpful member thereof, as soon as he became old enough.

When about twelve years old and the family lived on the bank of the Ohio river, in Virginia, he had the privilege of boating, which he greatly enjoyed and probably spent there the happiest year of his life.

In 1846, with consent of his mother and step-father, he went with his sister, Mary, to Belmont Co., O., where his two brothers, Amos and Levi, lived. Here he lived about a year, working part of the time at low wages and going to school part of the time. He then went to his uncle Samuel's, in Morgan Co., O., and worked part of his place and turned wooden bowls part of the time. Then worked in a saw mill on Wolf Creek, with Wm. Pierpoint, one year. In the spring of 1850, in company with his sister, Mary, and her husband, D. G. Ellis, he moved to Linn Co., Iowa.

Here an arrangement was made for him to go with his brother-in-law and his uncle Elihu Robins who each had a yoke of oxen, up into Blackhawk Co., and take "squatter's claims," and go to work breaking prairie and building for each.

But the first night after they arrived and pitched their tent, the oxen were stolen. They were not found until fall so they went back to Linn Co., and spent the summer there.

His uncle decided not to go again but he and Ellis went and got good claims with both timber and prairie land and water.

"Nearly all the settlers were living on government land and had a sort of "club law" for mutual protection. After they had worked awhile improving their claims, a fellow came along that thought he did not care for club law, and that it would be a nice thing to get improvements for nothing. So he "entered" both claims and bid defiance to the squatters club." "But the squatters gathered in from all over the county and made him a visit and after much persuasion and some threatening he agreed to give them up if he could get his money back. Neither of them had the money but found a man that was willing to take the claims and give the fellow the amount of his purchase money and pay them for their improvements, This gave them the means to enter other unimproved land which they did."

He married 1852-6-27, MARY ANN POYNER, daughter of a Baptist minister, who had taken a farm nearby. She was born 1834-7-24, near Crawfordsville, Ind. Her father, Nathan Poyner, was born 1791-12-8, in Georgia, Moved to Ohio. A soldier in the war of 1812. Moved to Indiana, at an early day and to Iowa, in 1847. Of Scotch Irish descent, died 1867-5-16. Her mother, Nancy Poyner, nee Johnson, was born 1794-5-16, in Kentucky, of Irish descent. Died 1854-4-20.

Hiram and wife stayed in Blackhawk Co., till the spring of 1858, when they moved to Coffee Co., Kansas.

This proved to be a bad move. He entered a beautiful piece of prairie land which had a rich soil but the subsoil was a hard pan and hence the vegetation could not endure the long droughts to which the country was then subject. He spent most of the means he had in improving the farm, worked six years and every year except one, failed to raise enough to support his family. He then sold out for a good deal less than the farm cost him and returned to Iowa, much broken in fortune and rented a farm in Linn Co., two years and then bought a farm "on time" in Blackhawk Co., and worked there till he paid about $1,000 in interest. But the interest and taxes were about all he could make beside keeping his family. Selling this place he went out into Nebraska, and filed a claim on a half-section of land under the "Homestead and Timber Clause Act." But about that time there were several years in succession in which that section of the country was overrun with grasshoppers, so that they were obliged to abandon their claim and never moved to it but went and settled in the little town of Akron, in Plymouth Co., Iowa. There they stayed 20 years. Some of the time he worked with a team; some of the time rented land near town and some of the time did carpenter work. Also kept a small furniture store a while, and did anything he could do to make a living and send his children to school.

His health became so badly broken that his physician advised him to go south. He sold out his little possession at Akron, and in early April, 1896, moved to Mississippi, near Canton, Madison Co. Here he gained in health but lost financially. The land he bought was so poor that he had to buy so much fertilizer he could not make farming pay.

They sold out there and December 1st, 1900, started for Oklahoma, in a covered wagon, intending to take a homestead if they could but there were more applicants than land. Had a long season of typhoid fever at Mountain View, Oklahoma, in the fall of 1901.

As soon as he was able to travel, they went up into Iowa, to visit their children, while he was regaining his health. In the spring of 1902, decided not to return to Oklahoma, but to go to Washington. Had part of their goods shipped to them and gave part away.

He wrote in a letter dated June 25, 1905: "Here we are in the foothills of the Cascade Mountains, holding down a homestead. Have very little of this world's goods, but if we can just manage to make a comfortable living till the Master says 'it is enough, come up higher,' it is all I am particular about. My wife and I have been members of the Methodist church for over 40 years and are trying to live Christian lives."

Has held several offices he did not think worth reporting until urged to do so, as township trustee, assessor and school director and in church, steward, trustee, s. s. superintendent, treasurer of building committee and in a Good Templars Lodge, about all the offices.

Politically he has been Whig, Republican, Prohibitionist.

He died at the home of his daughter, Amy Alice Ellis, in Salem, Oregon, November 21st, 1910. He was personally known to the writer as a very good and helpful boy in the home and it has been no surprise to learn in after years that he was a good and worthy man. An aged minister who had once been his pastor and who had known him for nearly thirty years, testified to his Christian character, steady-going habits and useful life.

Children:

61 NATHAN POYNER, born 1853-11-20.
11 MARY EMILY, born 1855-8-24, died 1857-9-15.
62 III MARY ALICE, born 1857-10-6.
IV LEVI SUMNER, born 1860-9-11, died 1862-10-10.
63 V JAMES ELMER, born 1864-1-7.
64 VI CELIA ANNETTE, born 1868-4-25.
65 VII CAROLINE ASENATH, born 1872-12-3.

33

WILLIAM (5). HAMPTON, (Zachariah 4, John 3, John 2, Joseph 1) was born 1826-3-14, near Pennsville, Morgan Co., O.

Was raised on a farm but also had a taste for learning. Remained at home on the farm with his parents till they moved to Iowa, in the fall of 1851, and went with them.

He married CHARITY WOOD, 1853-6-24, in Friends' meeting at Flushing, Belmont Co., O. She was a school-teacher and the daughter of Pusey and Charity Wood of Smithfield, O., where she had been born 1828-11-11. Was the youngest of nine children all of whom married and had children.

They went directly to Iowa. He had been teaching near Lisbon, Linn Co., and continued to do so till the spring of 1854, when they settled on the farm near Viola, same county, where they brought up their family.

Children:

I RUTH COPE, born 1855-2-22, died 1868-2-28. (13 years.)

II SARAH GRIFFITH, born 1856-3-16, died 1875-12-21. (nineteen and one- half years.)

66 III EMLEN, born 1857-12-7.

IV DAVID C., born 1859-9-11, died 1887-7-15. (twenty-eight years.)

V LYDIA ANN, born 1861-3-30, died 1885-7-14. (twenty-four and one-half years.)

67 VI MARY ELIZA, born 1863-9-26.

68 VII LEWIS PUSEY, born 1865-7-4.

VIII JOHN CLINTON, born 1867-4-3, died 1888-12-30. (twenty-one and two-thirds years.)

IX AMY RUTH, born 1868-2-6, died 1891-12-5.

X LOUISA MARY, born 1870-5-15, married to Atlin V. Stout, 1887, at home by Friends ceremony, died 1894-2-3, at the home of her father-in-law, Isaac Stout, near Viola.

XI ZACHARIAH W., born 1873-3-27, died 1905-2-19. "Studied Osteopathy" at Des Moines, and began practice at Ackworth. Was there less than a year when he contracted tuberculosis.

For want of data, only three of these children are treated separately. Their history is a sad one. All accounts agree in giving them high praise for moral and religious uprightness of life. Anna Hampton, who knew them all through the life time of most of them, says: "They were good children," and writes pathetically of them.

In answer to questions, one of the surviving ones, (Dr. Mary E.) writes: "I cannot give much data for publication concerning those whose memory is sacred to me but am glad to know their worth while they were with me and their reward is on high."

* See sixth generation.

Again in a letter she writes: "I am sorry I cannot do better about the incidents but there seems to be little for publicity. I could tell what others have said of some of the family, as that a friend said of sister Sarah: "The sight of her charmed me," she was so bright an example. Also of sister Anna, (Lydia Ann) Julia Otis of N. Y., said: "She was the most self-sacrificing girl I ever saw."

* "Chester Batty who was considered an authority, said of brother John: "I could not put my hand on his

equal." Brother Zachariah was noted for his kindness at school as well as at home. I can only say, I grew up surrounded with loving hearts which reminds me of the lines:

"Hand in hand with angels
Through the world we go."

CHARITY WOOD HAMPTON, the mother of these children, died 1903-12-31. (?). William outlived his wife, two years, died 1906-1-8, in Linn Co., Iowa. He was a farmer most of his life. A very zealous orthodox Friend of the small band called "Primitive" and politically a Prohibitionist.

34 RUTH COPE (5) HAMPTON, (Zachariah 4, John 3, John 2, Joseph 1) born 1828-1-2, in Morgan Co., O., near Pennsville.

She lived with her parents on the farm where she was born till the fall of 1851, when in her twenty-fourth year she moved with the family to Linn Co., Iowa, where she died 1853-9-13.

In my few visits at her father's after she had attained young womanhood, she greatly impressed me as possessed of a really beautiful character, both spiritually and intellectually and apparently more thoughtful than many at her age.

Few and rare as those visits were, the memory of them has been helpful to me all through the nearly sixty years that have passed. An incident related in a letter she sent the writer from Iowa, reveals her character. On the evening before they were to leave the old home in Ohio, forever, she went down to the family spring near the house, and there in the silence of the evening, knelt and prayed. She was a lover of good poetry.

35 SARAH GRIFFITH (5) HAMPTON, (Zachariah 4, John 3, John 2, Joseph 1) born 1832-5-18, near Pennsville, Morgan Co., O.

Received a common school education and "attended a select school at Chesterfield, for a while." Was married to John P. Carbee, near Viola, Ia., 1853-6-12.

She lost her membership among the Friends by marrying "out of meeting," and never joined any church but said she sympathized with the Friends.

JOHN P. CARBEE was a son of John and Anna Carbee, of New Hampshire. Was born on a farm in Bath, Grafton Co., N. H., 1823-5-3. Received a common school education and lived with his parents until twenty-one years of age and then worked out on a farm one year. Going to Vermont, he continued to labor by the month till 1850. During that year he went to Linn Co., Ia., and on May 16th, entered 300 acres of government land located in sections 5 and 8 in Brown township.

He was elected a representative in the general assembly of the state of Iowa, in 1863, and re-elected in 1865, serving till 1867. While a member of the assembly, he served on many important committees and was also one of the signers of the resolution ratifying the amendment to the constitution of the United States, abolishing slavery.

He held all the offices in the gift of his fellow townsmen, except constable and township clerk.

Occupation farming, politics Republican.

"He was brought up a Congregationalist but did not unite with any church in Iowa, and died 1893-10-25. Sarah continued to live on the farm.

Children of Sarah G. (Hampton) Carbee:

I ANNA CARBEE, born 1856-12-8, married Robert Bailey, 1875-12-25. Child, Fred M., born 1879-10-5. Fred married Bessie Day, 1904-11-30.

II IDA CARBEE, was born 1859-8-8, married Walter Pearson, 1884-5-28. Child, WALTER LEIGH, born 1889-5-5.

III HATTIE L. CARBEE, born 1865-7-7, married Isaiah Pearson, 1875-7-7, who was a brother to Walter above, and born 1861-10-7.

Children of Hattie L. and Isaiah Pearson:

1. FRANK CARBEE, born 1886-11-11.
2. NETTIE, born 1888-4-29.
3. GEORGE JOHN, born 1891-10-20.

IV JOHN WILLIAM CARBEE, was born 1868-6-12, and married Alice Gordon, 1889-5-8.

Children of John William and Alice Carbee:

1. JOHN MELVIN, born 1890-9-24.
2. SAMUEL CHARLES, born 1891-12-30.
3. WILLIAM CLARENCE, born 1894-8-25.
4. ANNA VELMA, born 1896-3-18.
5. EUGENE, born 1901-3-5.

6 and 7. WILMER and WILMA, twins, born 1902-9-22.

V HENRY CLAY CARBEE, born 1873-10-5.

36

MARY ELMA (5) HAMPTON, (Zachariah 4, John 3, John 2, Joseph 1) born 1835-2-8 near Pennsville, Morgan Co., O. Moved with parents to Linn Co., Ia., in 1851. On the 18th of the 7th month, 1855, in Friends meeting, at Viola, was married to PEARSON EMBREE, son of Joseph and Rebecca (Clendenning) Embree, born 1829-9-23, in Morgan Co., O., died 1900-11-29, at Kansas City, Mo. She died 1890-7-16, in Florida.

They lived in Linn, Butler and Jefferson Counties, Ia. Went to Kansas in 1884 and later to Florida.

The following items are taken from a paper sent to the editor which appears to have been copied from a memoir of Mary Elma's husband.

"PEARSON EMBREE."

"Delicate in health, his was a hard struggle for life. In the fall of 1862, he moved to Springfield, Ia., and became postmaster. Also had a small store. At the close of the war he sold out his store and moved out of town for a year, when he moved back to take charge of the post office in which position, he remained till 1872. About 1868, he was converted and joined the Methodist Episcopal church at Springfield. December 4th, 1869, he was licensed to preach. In due course he was ordained local deacon and afterward local elder.

"In 1872, he went to Butler Center Circuit where he served one year, and then went into the Bible Work. In July, 1873, he was overcome with heat from which he never recovered but remained a great sufferer the remainder of his days."

Children of Mary Elma (Hampton) Embree.

I CHARLES SUMNER EMBREE, was born 1856-5-7, at Viola, Ia., and married in 1885-3-19, at Council Grove, Kansas, SALLIE D. REGAN, born 1866-3-20, near West Milton, Miami Co., O. Her father, Thomas Regan, son of Zadoc Regan, was born 1828-1-8, of Welch ancestry. In youth, Thomas Regan, was a member of the New Light church, but later a Congregationalist. A farmer.

Her mother's maiden name was Mary Ann Pearson, daughter of Enoch J. and Mary (Weeks) Pearson and born 1830-12-22. This Mary Weeks was a daughter of Benjamin and Abagail Weeks.

Charles Sumner and wife moved to Bonifice, Florida, in November, 1885. He began preaching in 1890, in Florida, was ordained in 1891, in the Congregational church. "Came back to the Methodist Episcopal church South, in 1898, at Meridian, Miss., and served as pastor at Walnut Grove, Cocran, Mathersville and Fannin, all in Mississippi. Came into the Methodist Episcopal Church at Choctaw, Oklahoma, in 1904. Served at Choctaw and was serving at Yelton, Oklahoma, in 1909.

"Is a local elder and does supply work." Takes a deep interest in family history and is gathering information about the Hamptons, Embrees and Regans.

Children of Charles Sumner Embree:

1. ARCHIE R., born 1886-1-2, in Florida.
2. CARL H., born 1890-1-26, in Florida.
3. ROY J., born 1894-2-28, died 1895-3-30, in Florida.
4. EDNA MAY, born 1903-11-10, in Mississippi.

II EZRA BENJAMIN EMBREE, born 1861-6-11, at Viola, Ia. Married 1883-2-8, at Springville, Ia., ANNIE W. ENGLE, daughter of Caleb P. and Rhoda (Langstaff) Engle. She was born 1860-7-7. Lived at Springville and Olewine, Ia. Moved to Kansas in 1900.

Children of Ezra Benjamin Embree:

1. ETHEL MAY, born 1884-5-25.
2. ARTHUR RAYMOND, born 1886-3-6.
3. GUY LUTHER, born 1887-11-21.
4. EDNA RHODA, born 1889-5-20.
5. HARLEY CALEB, born 1890-8-?
6. JOHN PEARSON, born 1892-12-17.
7. CLARA MARIA, born 1896-1-12.

They were divorced in 1896, at Marion, Ia. He married 2nd, on 1898-10-10, at Olewine, Ia., Ida E. Spencer, born 1869-4-7.

Children by 2nd wife:

1. MARY IRENE, born 1899-12-24.
2. IDA AMELIA, born 1901-7-22.
3. ELMA CATHARINE, born 1903-3-11.
4. WILMA MAY, born 1904-7-13.

Carpenter. Republican.

III SYLVIA MAY, born 1863-5-21, at Springville, Ia., married 1889, at Springville, to James Adison Gilbert, born 1857-10-1, at Southland, O., son of Joal and Mary Gilbert.

Lived at Paralto, Ia., till 1895, Minneapolis, Minn.,

till 1899, when they moved to Kansas City.?

Railroad man. Republican. Friend.

Children of Sylvia May:

1. ORVILLE JOEL GILBERT, born 1892-9-17.
2. MARY GRACE GILBERT, born 1899-6-15.

IV JOHN S., born 1865-8-28, died 1866-8-19.
V JOSEPH, born 1870-9-11, died 1871-2-8.

VI JAMES ORVILLE EMBREE, born 1880-4-27.

Educated in common schools, married Mittie Edna Palmer, at Mathersville, Miss., 1906-12-17, daughter of Joseph and Martha Omelia (Martin) Palmer. Father raised at Denham, Miss., and mother at Sherbuta, Clark Co., Miss.

Since marriage, James Orville and wife, have lived at Mathersville, Longford, and Laurel, Miss.

He is "a licensed local preacher in the Methodist Episcopal Church South. Has been Sunday School superintendent."

Wife is a member of the Baptist (missionary)church, and a Sunday School teacher.

He "stands state and national Prohibition of the liquor traffic."

Carpenter and farmer. Democrat.

37 MARTHA (5) HAMPTON, (Asa 4, John 3, John 2, Joseph 1) born 1828-9-8, in Belmont Co., O., lived with her parents in several places in Ohio and went with them to Linn Co., Ia., as related in Asa's history. Married 1851-8-19, at Mt. Vernon, to ALBERT TAYLOR, born 1827-5-8, in Richland Co., O. "His parents died when he was small and he had no records of any kind." His daughter did not know his parents' names.

They lived first on a farm near Mt. Vernon, then moved in the fall, 1855, it is thought to Blackhawk Co., and lived on a farm between Raymond and Waterloo.

Here Martha died 1872-8-31, buried in Poyners cemetery.

I remember her as a very good, patient, helpful girl to her mother and the family. She did a great deal of work and had "a world of care" of the younger ones.

She was raised a Friend among whom she had a "birth right," but lost it by marrying "out of unity" and joined the Baptists.

My mother's record says, "she raised a well ordered family."

Her husband outlived her seventeen and one-half years. Part of the time on a farm, he owned, near Wolsey, S. D., but in later years, with his daughter, Mary Louisa, on one of his farms, near Raymond, Ia., died 1890-3-23, and buried in Poyner's cemetery.

Baptist. Democrat.

Children of Martha (Hampton) Taylor:

I MARY LOUISA TAYLOR, born 1853-1-7, in Linn Co., Ia., married James Harvey Douglas, 1874-12-23, at Raymond, Iowa.

Children of Mary Louisa:

1. OLIVER E., born 1875-9-24.
2. ELRA T., born 1878-8-20.
3. EARL R., born 1884-2-18.
4. WALTER A., born 1896-8-25.

II SYLVESTER CLARIDON TAYLOR, born 1857-7-27, near Raymond, Blackhawk Co., Ia., married Mary Barton, at Raymond, 1882-9-8. Moved to Wolsey, S. D., April (?), and remained there until March, 1902. Then returned to Waterloo, Ia., where he was living in September, 1907.

Children of Sylvester C. Taylor:

1. ANNA, born 1883-9-23.
2. BLANCH, born 1889-4-23.

III ASENATH LUCELLA TAYLOR, born 1860-9-10, near Raymond, Ia., married Charles Cummings Gaston, 1882-11-12. Moved to Covert, Osborn Co., Kansas, and lived there until March 15th, 1894. Then moved back to Waterloo, Ia.

Children of Asenath L., born in Covert, Kansas.

1. MABEL LENORA GASTON, born 1885-2-1.
2. ETHEL MAY GASTON, born 1888-1-11.
3. HOWARD TAYLOR GASTON, born 1890-2-13.

38

BENJAMIN FRANKLIN (5) HAMPTON, (Asa 4, John 3, John 2, Joseph 1) born 1831-11-22, in Ohio, probably in Belmont Co., and lived with his parents in various places in that state, as related in the history of Asa, and moved with them to Mt. Vernon, Ia., in the spring of 1850. A little later went to Cedar Rapids, same county, and made his home, his brother James, says, with his aunt, Mary Ann Robins and her husband, "for some years" before marriage, which was about four years after going to Iowa. Helped his uncle in making brick. 1854-8-3, (wife said 1853 but changed it to Aug. 3, 1854, married CAROLINE AMELIA SHIPMAN, at Cedar Rapids. She had taught school several terms before to marriage. Was the daughter of Oran E. and Harriett (Griswald) Shipman. They were natives of New York. Oran was a member of the Disciple or "Christian" church and Harriett was a Methodist. A little later Caroline's parents moved to Waterloo, Ia., where her father kept a confectionary store and a meat market. He was at one time Mayor of Waterloo, and was also Trustee of the Poor.

Benjamin and his bride, first went to housekeeping on his mother, Esther Hampton's, farm, a few miles from Fairview and 20 miles from Cedar Rapids, where they remained two years and then moved to Waterloo, Blackhawk Co. There they owned a house and lot which they traded to Hiram Hampton for a 40 acre farm nearby, where they lived, she says, three years. Then moved to Shellsbury, in Benton Co. Here they both joined the Presbyterian church.

Benjamin's occupation after marriage, was farming and teaming. A Republican. In September 1862, enlisted in Reg. 28, Co. D., Iowa V. I.

The regiment was organized at Iowa City, 40 miles away where they remained three months. There his wife with some friends, visited him, taking her youngest child, little Gertrude, then in her third year, with her. "Young as she was she could pick out her father among the 1400 uniformed men there," her mother writes and "sang a song, carrying the tune though she could not talk plain." "It made some of the soldiers shed tears thinking of their own little ones at home."

He was given a furlo twice during his time of nearly two years service and they were the only times his family saw him afterward. His brother, James, says: "He was one who scaled the walls at Fort Donelson. Had his haversack shot away, a minnie ball striking his gun. He then charged the enemy with bayonet but came out without a scratch himself."

Later he took sick at New Orleans, and died July 7th, 1864. He was buried in the National cemetery at New Orleans.

His wife wrote, "I think he was a true Christian." His brother James and wife, Alice Irving Hampton, report that they visited Chalmetto cemetery in the spring of 1906, and found Benjamin's grave near the large monument.

Children:

69 I ADALINE ADELIA, born 1857-10-5.

70 II ESTELLA VICTORIA, born 1859-1-10.

71 III GERTRUDE, born 1860-5-12.

IV WILLIAM, born 1862-2-16. Lived two weeks.

Caroline Shipman Hampton, the mother of these

children, was left a widow when the oldest was not yet 7 years old. She had their house and lot in Shellsbury, and says she "had a pension of $8.00 a month and $2.00 a month for each child till they were sixteen. Sewed for other people, kept her children in school and kept them together."

Writes tenderly of Benjamin and his brother, James, who "was very good to her and helped her quite a little." She had as she says a busy time with three children to care for, but also had the great satisfaction that they were good children.

After over nine years of widowhood, she was married 1873-9-14, to Daniel Sphan, with whom she lived over 27 years. He died 1900-11-22. He was a carpenter and they went to housekeeping at Vinton and then went to Tipton, Cedar Co., Ia., and from Tipton to Brighton, Washington Co., where she wrote on October 4th, 1907, she "had been living 15 years." She had "two children by her second husband, a daughter, Agnes Sphan, who was living near and a son, Edwin Sphan, who died at the age of four."

She lost her pension by remarrying, but after her second husband's death it was restored at $12 per month.

39 ELI GRIFFITH (5) HAMPTON, (Asa 4, John 3, John 2, Joseph 1) born 1833-5-10, probably in Belmont Co., O. Lived with his parents several places in Ohio and moved with them as related in their history to Linn Co., Ia., in spring of 1850.

Married 1853-10-6, at Mt. Vernon, Ia., ELMIRA ISHAM. He conducted a livery stable quite successfully for a number of years, sold out and bought a farm five miles from Cedar Rapids, where he lived till 1873, after which he lived on a farm belonging to his brother, James, near Cedar Falls, in Hardin Co. He then bought a farm of 400 or 450 acres in Beuna Vista Co., near Marathon, where he kept a large number of cattle and farmed extensively.

He died 1892-5-5, at Storm Lake, Ia. "Never departed

from the faith of the Friends." "Left an estate worth $20,000."

Children:

72 I OLIVER ASA, born 1854-11-9.
73 II WILLIAM ALLEN, born 1856-4-11.
74 III LINDLEY E., born 1859-1-5.
IV ARTHUR EDWARD, born 1861-5-2, died 1871-4-25.
V GEORGE T., born 1863-1-8, died 1863-9-3.
75 VI JESSE JAMES, born 1865-10-5.
76 VII CHARLES HENRY, born 1869-5-28.
77 VIII CLARA BELLE, born 1873-6-22.
78 IX ERNEST ELMER, born 1876-9-13.

His wife after nearly eleven years of widowhood, married to Wm. Burgess, 1903-2-9, and resided at Iowa Falls, until her death 1906-5-7. Buried in Iowa Falls cemetery. "She was a faithful and attentive member of the Congregational church of that place."

40 JAMES W. (5) HAMPTON, (Asa 4, John 3, John 2, Joseph 1) born 1835-1-24, he thinks at Pennsville, Morgan Co., O. Lived with his parents at several places in Morgan, Athens and Washington counties, going with them to Linn Co., Ia., in the spring of 1850. (See their history). From a little passed four years old, till nineteen, he lived the life of a farmer's boy, his father giving his sons their freedom at nineteen. "James began business by breaking prairie with five yoke of oxen in the summer of 1854. He bought the oxen on credit and sold them in the fall, his summer's work making him $350."

"In November he entered into partnership with Ulysses Doan and they opened a store at Fairview, Jones Co., Ia. After a few months, selling out to his partner, he joined his uncle, Samuel B. Hampton, in erecting a sawmill on the latter's farm near Viola. Not feeling satisfied with milling and eager to enter again into the mercantile business, he sold his interest in October,

1855, to Wm. Doan, for $1100 and went to Waterloo, Blackhawk Co., bought a lot for $100, built a house and started a store there in 1855, on a small capital. Goods were bought in Chicago, shipped to Davenport, 140 miles from Waterloo, and hauled out there in wagons. He did well and sold out two years later for $2,300." While here married SUSANNAH TEDROW, at Trenton, Ia., 1855-12-9.

"After selling out at Waterloo, he went on a tour of investigation for another place to locate, passing through northern Missouri and southern Iowa. He finally settled at Liberty, Clarks Co., Ia., in the fall of 1857, where he opened another store and in connection with it bought and sold farm stock which he drove 80 miles to Ottumwa, the nearest railroad station and shipping point, then the terminus of the Burlington road.

"In 1861, the store and all his goods were burned, leaving him indebted to Chicago merchants, $3500."

"He continued his stock dealing which became extensive. His last drove of hogs shipped in 1863, numbered 2200. In these two years he had made enough to pay his debts and had $3,800 to commence business again."

In 1863, he went to Mt. Pleasant, Henry Co., Ia., where he purchased a three story brick store house for $2,200, went to Chicago, with his $1,600 and purchased goods to the amount of $9,000, mostly on time. "In 1866 he bought the former home of Bishop Hamlin, in Mt. Pleasant, which became the family home while in Iowa."

"In the winter of 1885, he had a severe attack of pneumonia, contracted on a trip to the Gulf of Mexico. His health was so broken that he retired from business in March."

"In October, 1887, their home at the Bishop Hamlin house was burned down and he went with his wife and two daughters to California in seach of health for him. Not finding the climate suited to him they returned as far as Denver, Colo., in Feb., 1888.

Here he built a house and Denver has continued to be his home. On 1902-4-29, his wife, Susannah Tedrow

Hampton, died after a short illness though she had not been well for many years. Born in Somerset Co., Penn., 1834-8-12. At the age of six years, was moved with her parents, to Athens Co., O. In 1854, with three brothers, moved to Trenton, Henry Co., Ia. Was the daughter of Joseph and Barbara Ann (Geist) Tedrow. Joined the Methodist Episcopal church in 1865 or 1866. "Lead a quiet life and did not participate much in the work of the church."

Children:

79 I EMMA LODISKA, born 1857-9-23.
80 II ELLA ALWILDA, born 1860-2-29.
81 III HATTIE ANNETTA, born 1863-12-15.

"Some moths after the death of his wife, James, with his daughter, Ella A. Gregg, and her husband, and their daughter, started on a tour of the Holy Land, Jan. 1903. Of this he wrote an interesting account. The trip beside Palestine, included a visit to the Maderia Islands, the principal parts of the Medeterranian from Gibraltar to Constantinople, Egypt, as far up the Nile as old Memphis, Greece, Italy, Switzerland, Paris and London. And last but not least interesting to them, no doubt, was the experience of a terrific storm at sea on the return voyage, taking 28 life boats off the ship and delaying their arrival at New York, two days."

James married 1905-1-25, MARY ALICE IRVING, aged 55, born 1849, in Columbia Co., Penn., near Bloomburg, daughter of Joseph and Christianna (Billig) Irving.

At the age of 13, Alice united with the Lutheran church, at Bloomburg. "Her father and mother were very earnest Christians and faithful members of the same church."

In 1877, Alice went to Scranton, Pa., to live and there united with the Presbyterian church, where she was very active. On going to Denver she united with the Central Presbyterian church and has been a faithful member ever since. (3-3-1908.) They spent their first winter after marriage in California. In the winter of 1906, they went to Florida and the Bahama Islands and in the winter of 1907, visited Italy, France, Switzerland and England. Built a new home in Denver, into which they moved, 1907-12-24. Although counting himself as retired from business in 1885, yet he wrote 3-3-1908, that he had built since located in Denver, four very good houses, two of them being hotels.

He joined the Methodist Episcopal church at Mt. Pleasant, Ia., but wrote in 1908, that his then wife, was such a good worker in the Presbyterian church, that he was attending that church.

Says, "I am a Republican from a way back."

41 JESSE (5) HAMPTON, (Asa 4, John 3, John 2, Joseph 1) born 1843-9-19, near Plymouth, Washington Co., O. Moved with his parents to Linn Co., Ia., spring of 1850. As a child he was active. The word "spry" may not be classic English, but I know of no word to describe him better at the time I knew him.

Although very young for such an enterprise, he was associated about 1857, with John Brown (Ossowatomie Brown) and James Lane ("Jim Lane") in their resistence of the slave holding propagandists, known as "The Border Ruffians," who terrorized and slaughtered the "Free State" settlers of Kansas.

Jesse's Quaker ancestry and associations had made him an ardent hater of slavery but had failed to take the fight out of him. After that he returned to his old home in Linn Co. When the civil war began, although under age, he enlisted in Reg. 13, Iowa V. I. Co., A. Was in several battles, the most eventful one being that of Pittsburg Landing or Shiloh, April 6th and 7th, 1862. He was on the battlefield 24 hours. Early in the morning of April 7th, he was wounded, having three fingers of his right hand shot off and a musket ball wound in his abdomen. He was sent home as soon as his wounds were cared for at the hospital at Mound City, near the mouth of the Ohio river. But his brother, James, having received news of the battle and seeing Jesse's name in the list of wounded, in a newspaper, started for the first train he could get, 80 miles distant.

Not knowing where to find him he stood at the gangway at Keokuk, while they unloaded three vessels of wounded soldiers, but his brother, Jesse, was not among them. He then went to St. Louis and searched six different hospitals. Not finding him he went to Cairo and searching, to no purpose, went to Mound City, where he learned Jesse had been cared for and sent home.

On arriving at home, Jesse first went to his brother Eli's, at Mt. Vernon, but soon after to James' home at Liberty, Clarke Co. After recovering sufficiently, he joined in partnership with James in buying and herding cattle for a short time but he never fully recovered from the effects of the wound and in a year afterward, was taken suddenly ill and died after three days illness, 1863-4-9. He was buried at Liberty, Clarke Co., Ia., where his grave is marked with a stone with coat of arms. Unmarried.

42

BETHULA ANN (5) HAMPTON, (Asa 4, John 3, John 2, Joseph 1) born 1846-4-30. She chose to be called Anna and so wrote her name and was so known by her friends. Lived with her parents near Plymouth, O., till they moved to Iowa., in the spring of 1850.

A little before the end of her eighth year, death deprived her of a father's loving care and three years and a day later, of a mother's also. She then lived several years with her sister, Martha, near Waterloo, Iowa. When a little past seventeen she went to her brother, James' home, in Mt. Pleasant, Ia., and attended the Iowa Wesleyan University.

At about sixteen she began teaching which she continued for about ten years or until her marriage except when going to school herself. She first taught near Waterloo, then near Mt. Pleasant and later in the graded schools of Mt. Pleasant.

One day before twenty-six years old, 1872-4-29, she

married DANIEL A. RISSER, born 1844-4-28, at Cuyahoga Falls, O., son of Jacob and Barbara Risser. Over 19 years later and after a residence of 28 years at Mt. Pleasant, moved with her husband and children to Lincoln, Neb., 1891-8-29. While attending school at Mt. Pleasant, she was elected a member of P. E. O. college society.

When about sixteen, she joined the Methodist Episcopal church, became a Sunday School teacher and a member of the Woman's Foreign Missionary Society. Was president of this society at St. Pauls church, Lincoln, Neb., after moving there. She "delivered two public addresses, one at Mt. Pleasant and one at Lincoln. Both were on women's influence on Christian work in foreign fields."

Children of Bethula Ann (Hampton) Risser:

I MAUD HAMPTON RISSER, born 1873-11-2, at Mt. Pleasant, Ia. Attended the public schools and entered the Iowa Wesleyan University there as a music student of the piano and graduated from the conservatory of music of the college at the age of seventeen. She was also a member of the P. E. O. society of the college. "After moving to Lincoln she entered the Nebraska State University as a regular student and was elected a member of the Kappa Kappa Gamma Society."

"She also studied music under Sherwood, of Chicago, and at the writing of her mother's last letter, April 1906, "was practicing her profession."

II GEORGE HAMPTON RISSER, born 1877-3-20, at Mt. Pleasant, Ia. While living there he attended the public schools and was also a student in the Iowa Wesleyan University and a member of the Homline Literary Society."

"After moving to Lincoln, he entered the Nebraska State University, as a law student and graduated from that department in June, 1897, at the age of twenty but under the law of Nebraska, could not receive his diploma till 21 years of age."

While in the University he was elected a member of the Sigma Chi Society, a college fraternity and also a member of the Phi Delta Phi society, a legal fraternity and also a member of the Palladion Literary Society.

A vacancy occured in the office of Justice of the Peace which he was appointed to fill and in April, 1906, he was filling his second election term in the same.

1899-11-15, married Lulu West, of Wyoming, Neb. At date of report, (April, 1906) had a daughter, Marion.

43

OLIVER LIVZEY (5) HAMPTON, (John 4, John 3, John 2, Joseph 1) born 1831-3-2, in Belmont Co., O., and lived with his parents in that county and in Morgan and Athens counties, as recorded in their lives, (See John 4.) going with them to Iowa, in spring of 1854.

On 1857-4-22, married HANNAH GREGG, daughter of Caleb and Milicent Gregg. Her father was a minister among the Friends. Oliver and wife lived several years in the neighborhood of Hopewell Friends church, near Viola and Springville, Ia. He entered land after going to Iowa, but sold it and bought a farm nearby. He learned the carpenter's trade in Ohio and followed it all through life at times but farmed mostly. Had great love for fruit culture. He adhered to the Friends' church in which he was born, took great interest in the society where he lived and "held several important offices in the church." Was not much engaged in politics." "Was a quiet, good, pleasant, Christian man, loved by all," his sister says "as far as I know."

His education was rather limited. Was at Mt. Pleasant, (?) Ohio, Boarding School, one term, beside common schools.

Children:

82 I DANIEL WILLIAMS, born 1858-1-4.

II EMMA, born 1861-6-20, died 1873-2-28.

III ELMER, born 1866-6-8, died 1866-8-12.

IV NELLY, born 1868-10-4, died 1869-1-17.

83 V DELWIN C., born 1872-10-18.
VI EVELINE, born 1879-7-2, died 1884-6-28.
84 VII WILBUR, born 1884-8-20.

Oliver died 1899-1-9. His wife still living, Feb., 1910.

44

SARAH WILLIAMS (5) HAMPTON, (John 4, John 3, John 2, Joseph 1) born 1832-12-2, at Pennsville, Morgan Co., O., she thought, and lived with her parents at Chesterfield, then Athens Co., and later near Barnsville, Belmont Co., O. Here at Ridge Meeting House by Friends ceremony 1852-4-8, married RICHARD MOTT, born at Sunsburg, O., and son of William and Sarah (Edgerton) Mott, the former from Trenton, N. Y., and the latter from (North) Carolina. Both ministers of the society of Friends. She moved overland to Linn Co., Ia., in spring of 1854, with husband, infant son, parents and family.

Removed in 1858 to Cedar Co., Ia., and in 1865 to Jones Co., Ia. For two and one-half years, ending in 1885, she was matron with her husband as superintendent at Friends Boarding School, Barnesville, O. They also held the same position at Scattergood Seminary, a Friends' school, near West Branch, Ia., for four terms, ending in 1894.

She adhered to the Friends (orthodox) among whom she had a birth right. Held the office of overseer for a number of years and about 1880, was appointed elder which station she continued to hold. She was evidently faithful in training her children. Her sister says Sarah's children are being well educated and that none of them nor their father nor grandfathers have ever used either tobacco or intoxicating liquors.

She died 1909-8-10.

Children of Sarah (Hampton) Mott:

I JOHN WM. MOTT, born 1853-1-17, married Sina A. Hall, at Stillwater, O., 1882-9-21, born 1856-2-28.

Children of John William Mott:

1. EDITH SARAH, born 1884-6-13, married Ray Newtin, 1905-10-25, one child, Arthur.

2. WALTER F., born 1887-5-8.

3. RACHEL, born 1889-12-26. In school at Barnesville, 1908.

4. JESSE D., born 1894-6-15.

II THOMAS EDGERTON MOTT, born 1854-8-18, married Martha Briggs, at Sunsburg, O., 1878-9-27.

Children of Thomas E. Mott:

1. RACHEL, born 1879-8-24, died 1882-9-30, in Ohio while there with her parents attending yearly meeting.

2. JOSEPH, born 1880-12-28, clerk at Beach Hotel, Atlantic City, N. J. Unmarried, January, 1908.

3. RICHARD H., 1885-10-11.

III JAMES MOTT, born 1857-6-11, married Emma Frances Warring, at Warmick, Ontario, Canada, 1891-3-12.

Children of James Mott:

1. EDGAR W., born 1892-12-6, died 1893-2.
2. ELLA E., 1893-12-24.
3. ETHEL CELIA, born 1895-3-17, died 1895-8-13.
4. SINA AMANDA, born 1896-3-29.
5. FRANCIS EDWARD, born 1897-12-27.
6. ANNA BEULA, born 1900-11-30.
7. JAMES LESLIE, born 1902-12-3, died 1903-3-8.
8. MARJORIE IRENE, born 1904-1-4.

IV MARY MOTT, born 1860-3-1, married William Penn Young, at Hopewell, near Viola, Ia., 1880-9-20.

Children of Mary (Mott) Young:

1. WILMER YOUNG, born 1887-10-20.
2. FLORENCE YOUNG, born 1892-9-19.
3. ANNA LORENA YOUNG, born 1894-5-31.
4. ARTHUR YOUNG, born 1903-2-2.

V DANIEL MOTT, born 1861-8-27, married Martha Bye, at Hickory Grove, near West Branch, Ia., 1891-11-11.

Children of Daniel Mott:

1. ALBERT D., born 1893-2-2, died 1894-1-27.
2. EDWARD EVERETT, born 1896-10-24.
3. BERTHA EMILY, born 1897-2-7, died 1899-9-18.
4. EDWIN, born 1900-1-31, died 1900-12-8.
5. CHARLES IRVING, born 1901-10-10.
6. ALFRED L. E., born 1903-6-15.
7. MABEL DOROTHY, born 1906-11-16.

VI ANNA MOTT, born 1864-10-27, married Samuel Hall, at Hopewell, near Viola, Ia., 1892-5-24.

Children of Anna (Mott) Hall:

1. TACY M. HALL, born 1895-3-31.
2. WILLIAM R. HALL, born 1897-7-6.
3. SARAH M. HALL, born 1900-5-15.

VII ELEANOR MOTT, born 1867-5-12, died 1868-4-19.

VIII CHESTER MOTT, born 1869-1-15, married Joanna Bowles, at Spring River, Kansas, 1899-9-22.

Children of Chester Mott:

1. MARY E., born 1900-12-22.
2. MILFORD, born 1905-7-28.
3. PAUL GILBERT, born 1906-2-7, died 1906-2-15.

IX ARTHUR HOWELL MOTT, born 1874-1-20, married Caroline Embree at Whittier, Ia., 1900-5-22.

Children of Arthur Howell Mott:

1. ERWIN LESTER, born 1903-11-3.
2. GERTRUDE, born 1905-2-12.

45 ROBERT WILLIAMS (5) HAMPTON, (John 4, John 3, John 2, Joseph 1) born 1835-6-13, probably at Pennsville, Morgan Co., O. Lived with parents at Chesterfield and at "The Ridge" near Barnsville, Belmont Co., and moved with them to Linn Co., Ia., in 1854. 1865-4-19, married ANNA BUNDY, born 1839-3-3, near Colrane, Belmont Co., O., daughter of Benjamin Bundy, born in N. Carolina and Delitha (Bailey) Bundy, born in Virginia. They settled on an 80 acre prairie farm near Springville, Linn Co., Ia. Later added 80 acres to their farm and continued to live on it 29 years. In the summer of 1895, they built a house in Whittier and moved there that fall where they were yet living at date or report, 1906.

Like many other good men, Robert, "thinks he was fortunate in choosing a wife." Says, "she has a literary taste, is a noble good woman and truly a 'home maker.'" They "gave their children a fair education."

Children:

85 I CHARLES CLYDE, born 1866-6-21.
86 II EDGAR CLIFTON, born 1867-12-19.
87 III CHESTER LARUE, born 1869-10-20.
88 IV MARY DELITHA, born 1874-2-22.
89 V WALTER JOHN, born 1888-8-31.

46 LUCINDA (5) HAMPTON, (John 4, John 3, John 2, Joseph 1), born 1837-6-23, at Chesterfield, then Athens, but now Morgan Co., O. Lived with parents in Ohio, and moved with them to Linn Co., Ia., in spring of 1854. Married DANIEL GREGG son of Caleb and Millicent Gregg, of Springville, Ia., 1855-4-18. He died 1857-10-12. One child was the issue of this union—ALFRED D. GREGG, born 1856-5-8, near Springville. He married Mary Eveline Hess, daughter of Jonathan and Nancy Hess, Viola, Ia., 1876-11-12. Their home, June, 1906, was Aitkin, Minn., where he was clerk in a store. In religiou they are Methodists.

Children of A. D. Gregg:

1. EUGENE GREGG, born 1881-5-28, married Hattie Mae Hazelton, daughter of D. C. Hazelton, 1903-1-17.
2. FRANK GREGG, born 1886-9-5.
3. IRMA GREGG, born 1890-10-4.

Lucinda was married 2nd to THOS. C. BATTY, 1862-1-22, son of Joseph Batty, of N. Y., born 1828-2-19. Educated at Westown Boarding School, Penn. She was his 2nd wife. "Was brought up according to the principles and testimonies of the Friends and was a firm believer in their doctrines. Her services were made considerable use of in conducting affairs of the church." "She endeavored to live in harmony with the teaching of Christ and to bring her children up in the nurture and admonition of the Lord." She was a good scholar for one having only the opportunity of a common school education.

"Because of her husband's going on appointed duty to labor among the Indians in the Indian Territory, in the 10th month, 1871, she was left with the entire care of the children and her son, only about 15 years of age, to work a farm of 80 acres. Many times she was obliged to wait weeks to hear from him, there being no railroad nearer than from one to two hundred miles away from him and the plains only crossed at intervals by mule teams. And he being out with the wild tribes many miles from any other white man, made her anxiety doubly great. He spent about three years with the Indians, roaming about with them, living in tents, eating such food as they ate, trying to teach them the ways of civilization and restrain them from making raids on the whites who lived on the borders of their country."

"His health became so broken that he returned to his

home and family, in the spring of 1874. He wrote a book entitled 'A Quaker Among the Indians,' which was published in 1875."

He gradually regained his health and lived on the farm till Lucinda's death, 1887-7-23. Her illness was several months duration which she bore with patience and resignation.

"He taught an Indian school again in 1889 and 1890, this time in Tama Co., Ia." In the spring of 1891, he moved to Mosk, Columbiana Co., O., and married Deborah Cadwalder, there, on the 4th month, 2nd, 1891. Died 1897-8-28.

He was an active member of the society of Friends, being at different times Clerk of the Monthly and Quarterly Meetings and also an overseer.

In politics, a Prohibitionist.

Children of Lucinda (Hampton) Batty:

I JOSEPH E. BATTY, born 1862-11-30, near Viola, Ia. Attended Barnesville Boarding School, 1883-4, married Mabel Outland, daughter of Joseph and Phebe Outland, of Barnesville, O., 1887-2-13. Lived in Iowa, till autumn of 1889. They went to Ohio. Home in June, 1906, was Pittsburg, Penn. Methodists. Prohibitionist.

Children of Joseph E. Batty:

1. WALTER DELBERT, born 1888-1-20.
2. MARTIN RUSSEL, born 1890-11-27.
3. WILLIAM HARLAN, born 1891-11-27.
4. JOHN HARMAN, born 1894-5-19.

II SARAH E BATTY, born 1864-9-18, near Viola, Ia., married 1884-11-18, Francis D. Hall, at Friends' meeting house, near Viola, son of John and Deborah S. (Davis) Hall of Barnesville, O., and born 1860-3-26. They lived the winter of 1884-5, with her grandparents, John and Mary Hampton, near Viola. Moved to Springville, Ia., near by which their home was in 1906. Occupation, farming. Religion, Friends Society.

Child of Sarah E. Batty Hall:

CLARA D. HALL, born 1885-11-10, graduated at Scattergood Seminary, 3rd month, 1904, married 1905-11-16, to Arthur R. Rockwell, son of Harvey and Mary Rockwell, of Paulina, O'Brian Co., Ia., where they lived in 1906. He was born 1878-10-22,

III MARY B. BATTY, born 1866-12-15, near Viola. Went to Friend's Boarding School, Barnsville, O., in 1883 and 1884 and to Tunescalla, N. Y., as assistant matron in the Indian school there in fall of 1887, and later as teacher in the same school. Left there 9-21-1893. Taught several terms of school elsewhere and was married 1901-4-3, to JOSEPH HENDERSON, of Paulina, O'Brian Co., Ia., son of Joseph and Isabella Henderson, of Canada. Their home (1906) is near Paulina, and occupation truck and fruit farming. Are active members of the Society of Friends, according to whose ceremony they were married.

Children of Mary B. (Batty) Henderson:

1. ALFRED J. HENDERSON, born 1902-7-6.
2. HERMAN FRANCES HENDERSON, born 1904-4-9.

IV HERMAN J. BATTY, born 1869-8-18. Attended Barnesville, O., Boarding School, winter of 1889-90. Graduated at Scattergood Seminary, 1894-3-15. Lived at Paulina, Ia. Votes for temperance and belongs to Friends church. Unmarried 1906. Carpenter.

V LUCINDA H. BATTY, born near Viola, 1871-10-5, during the raging of the Chicago fire. 1887-9 attended Barnesville, O., Boarding School. Spring of 1891, went to live with her father and stepmother at Mosk, Columbiana

Co. Married there 1893-8-24, to J. HOWARD EDGERTON, son of Jesse and Samira Edgerton, of that county. Farmers. Friends.

Children of Lucinda H. (Batty) Edgerton:

1. ALICE SAMIRA, born 1894-6-6.
2. CHESTER JESSE, born 1895-7-13.
3. RUTH, born 1897-9-4.
4. JOSEPH, born 1900-9-2.
5. DOROTHY, born 1902-4-23.
6. LUCINDA, born 1903-6-7.
7. MARY ELLEN, born 1905-10-?

VI MALINDA S. BATTY, born near Viola, 1875-9-14. "In the 3rd month, 1891, went to Mosk, O., to live with her father and stepmother."

Graduated at Barnesville Boarding School, 3-28-1895. Taught a few terms of school and married in 1898-4-15, to ELBERT LOREN COPE, son of Albert and Phebe (Ashton) Cope, of Dick, West Moreland Co., Penn. They lived a few years at that place and in 1902, moved to Columbiana Co., O. Farming and poultry raising. Friends. Prohibitionists.

Children of Malinda S. (Batty) Cope:

1. HOWARD HERMAN, born 1899-5-29.
2. CHESTER A., born 1901-9-9.

47 ANNA (5) HAMPTON, (John 4, John 3, John 2, Joseph 1) born in Belmont Co., O., 1840-4-3, and lived with her parents at several places near Barnesville, in that county, till the removal of the family to Linn Co., Ia., in 1854. She continued to live with her parents in the neighborhood of Viola, while they lived and then her home was with her sister, Sarah Mott and family, in the same community, till the summer of 1906, when she went with them to West Branch, Cedar Co., Ia.

She was evidently a very dutiful daughter. "Had most of the care of the home for quite a while," says, "I never had much school learning owing, to my great affliction in my speech which has been a very, very great trial to me of course, but I try to be resigned to my lot." "I feel in hopes many times, my life will not be an entire failure." "I have been a lifelong member of the orthodox Friends Society but never used very much. Was an overseer for a time in our little meeting." Speaking of her home with her sister and husband, she says: "I do enjoy it but it is not my own dear home and I spend many, many lonesome hours." Finally adds: "I have a soul to be saved or lost and hope and trust I may so live as to have a home in Heaven."

She took a lively interest in the preparation of this history and rendered much assistance in gathering materials for it. At a time when it looked doubtful whether sufficient data could be obtained for an intelligible and creditable history, because those who had expressed a desire to have the work done, yet neglected for month after month, for two or three years, to respond to appeals from the proposed editor for materials, Anna Hampton came to the rescue and sent, with encouraging words, a record her father had left of his family and ancestors. Without this timely help the work, after much talk, might have fallen through. This first help was followed up by many letters to the editor and to others of the Hampton family and relatives. Whatever success may be achieved in this undertaking, much of the credit will be due to Anna Hampton.

Her brother, Robert, writes: "Anna has led a rather obscure life, ever ready to administer to the needs and the comfort of others. She was faithful in caring for her aged parents and is now (7th mo. 26th, 1909) caring for her older sister who is slowly declining in health." "She has held some important offices in her church and has lived a very useful life." Unmarried.

48 ELIZA (5) HAMPTON, (John 4, John 3, John 2, Joseph 1) born 1844-4-5, in Belmont Co., O. Moved with parents in spring of 1854, to Linn Co., Ia. Married at Friends Meeting House near Viola, 1865-12-20, to JOSEPH CREW, son of Aquilla and Rachel (Farmer) Crew. He was born 1843-9-30 ,and died 1901-5-10.

After marriage they lived on a farm near Viola. In spring of 1870, moved to near Yankton, S. D., and took up a homestead, where they lived several years when the grasshoppers took their large good crops several times. Moved back to Linn Co., in fall of 1876, and lived on a farm awhile. Went to Marion, the county seat and conducted a boarding house for several years till her husband died. Her sister Anna wrote in 1905, that Eliza and her unmarried daughter have a very pretty home in Marion. She joined the Methodist Episcopal church while in S. Dakota, and is reported to be quite a church worker. "Had been treasurer of a Ladies Aid Society, for a number of years.

Children of Eliza (Hampton) Crew:

1 LAURA ALICE CREW, born 1867-4-20, Deputy in County Recorder's Office at Marion, Ia., June 1906.

II MARY ETHEL CREW, born 1876-5-3. A teacher until marriage. Married 1900-6-14, Dr. J. J. Booth, Marion, Ia. Has two children.

1. RONALD CLARK BOOTH, born 1901-9-8.
2. ROBERT JOSEPH BOOTH, born 1905-3-23.

49 LOVINA (5) HAMPTON, (John 4, John 3, John 2, Joseph 1) born 1846-6-27. Married to MAHLON BEDELL, 1866-12-19, at Hopewell Church. Child, Linda, born 1868-10-4, and died 1870-5-13.

They lived for a time on Oliver's farm while he moved into Springville, to have his boys attend school. The mother in feeble health, did not survive the death of her child quite one year. She died 1871-4-17. A good Christian spirited woman. The father Mahlon Bedell, died 1883-7-4.

50 EDWARD WILLIAMS (5) HAMPTON, (John 4, John 3, John 2, Joseph 1), born 1851-7-2, near Barnsville, O. Was moved with father's family to Linn Co., Ia., in 1854.

Opportunities for education, fairly good. Married 1872-11-18, Maria Ettie Morrison, at Muscatine, Ia., daughter of Henry Charles and Lucy (Batty) Morrison, and born at Lincoln, Vt. She was a granddaughter of Anna Batty, a well known minister of the Friends Society. Places of residence have been Iowa, Kansas, California, Nebraska and Colorado. Occupation, farming and canvassing missionary.

Member of Seventh Day Adventist Church. Republican but not a politician, taking no part in elections except where there is a moral issue. Wife wrote 8-5-1908, that she was an invalid and adds: "My long illness of more than 15 years has been a great disadvantage to the family in every way. My husband has stood by me nobly and has cared for my parents.

Children:

90 I CHARLES NEVIL, born 1877-4-19.
II JULIUS EDWARD, born 1879-8-18, died 1882-8-23.
91 III FRANK JULIUS, born 1883-2-24.

51 JONATHAN PIERPOINT (5) HAMPTON, (Samuel 4, John 3, John 2, Joseph 1), born 1832-5-30, in Morgan Co., O., lived with his parents in Ohio and went with them to Iowa, as related in the life of Samuel Betts (4) Hampton. Married Lydia Bundy, daughter of Jonathan and Achsa (Doudna) Bundy, 1854-11-14. Her parents were natives of N. Carolina. The Bundys were pioneers in Belmont Co., O.

Jonathan and Lydia lived near the Wapsapinnecon river for several years, moved to Cedar Co., for two years, then back to Linn Co., and in 1870, to Keokuk Co., where they had lived on a farm to date, 1906-6-4. Both were members of the Friends Society, and strongly attached to their doctrines and usages. In politics, Republican.

Children:

92 I JEPTHA, born 1855-8-20.
93 II LUCINDA M., born 1857-7-3.
94 III ADDA N., born 1859-5-12.
95 IV THOMAS ELWOOD, born 1861-12-20.
96 V ELIZABETH, born 1866-4-20.
97 VI SARAH E., born 1870-7-7.
98 VII JOHN W., born 1874-9-6.

52

MARY (5) HAMPTON, (Samuel Betts 4, John 3, John 2, Joseph 1) born 1836-10-15, in Chesterfield, then Athens, now Morgan Co., O. Lived there and in Penn Tp., with parents and went with them to Iowa. Most of her school days occurred at Chesterfield, some in Penn Tp., and very little in Iowa. 1854-12-1, married to EDWIN BEDELL, of Green Co., N. Y., where he was born, 1828-11-11. Both his parents orthodox Friends, and filling the station of elders therein.

Mary and husband had their first home in Jones Co., Ia. In May, 1865, moved to Duchess Co., N. Y., and had their home with his parents till October of that year, when they moved to Poughkeepsie, N. Y. Some time after this began keeping a boarding house which was continued 35 years till her husband's death, 1st mo., 16th, 1901.

In this work she was very successful. "Had a family of 20 to 30, mostly of persons who stayed with them a long time. One couple were with them 23 years. One widow 17 years. Some a few years only." "Somehow had the faculty of making a boarding house homelike to her boarders."

In religion, an orthodox Friend. "Had been a member of ministers and elders for 20 years" at date of report. "Overseer for several years previous to becoming a member of the select meeting."

Had also been a member of the W. C. T. U. for 20 years, occupying positions of responsibility on executive board and house committee." "Had been much interested in rescue work for last 10 years in the city (Poughkeepsie) a mission work, holding meetings every night where the drunkard and the outcast have been saved and led into a pure life. Served on the board of managers till the work was established when she withdrew from the more active duties but still attended the meetings where she was known as Mother Bedell."

In 1906, at the solicitation of her son and his wife, she went to live with them at Bayonne, N. J.

Children of Mary (Hampton) Bedell:

I EVALINDA BEDELL, born 1859-3-14, in Jones Co., Ia. Married to CHARLES HOWARD SPEAR, of Pitts-Pa., 1883-6-14. At an early age she manifested a great love and talent for instrumental music and was so eager to obtain a musical education that she would work early and late practicing on her piano. At the time of her death she was organist for a Presbyterian church in Pittsburg, to which she belonged.

She died May 30th, 1899. Her end was peaceful.

Children of Evalinda:

1 MARY ALINE SPEAR, born 1884-10-2. "Expected to complete a 4 year's course in Vassar College, in June, 1908. Stood well in her classes."

2. JAMES HOWARD SPEAR, born 1886-7-8. "Working in Westinghouse Electric concern, in 1907. Steady, of good habits, and much interested in church work."

3. HUDSON BEDELL SPEAR, born 1889-10-20. "Working in same place with brother in 1907. Steady and of good habits."

II CHARLES HAMPTON BEDELL, born 1861-12-18, in Jones Co., Ia. Interested in scientific studies. Graduated from Harvard College in Scientific Course. Entered Johns Hopkins University but left to accept a position of inspector of machinery with the Philadelphia Electric Dynamo Co., where he had been 18 years prior to June 1906. The factory came to be located at Bayonne, N. Y. Went to Quincy, Mass., Jan. 15th, 1908, to be chief engineer of Electric Boat Co.

Married Florence Gardner Whetstone, 1889-6-4, at Philadelphia.

Children of Charles H. Bedell:

1. MARION GARDNER BEDELL, born 1899-1-10.
2. CHARLES HAMPTON BEDELL, born 1905-9-6. Both at Swathmore, Penn.

III HULER E. BEDELL, born 1876-1-24. Poor health cut short his education. A severe cold ended in "hasty consumption," and he died in peace, May 9th, 1894.

53 ANN PIERPOINT (5) HAMPTON, (Samuel Betts 4, John 3, John 2, Joseph 1) born 1838-5-11, in Chesterfield, O. Lived with parents in Ohio and in Iowa. (See Samuel B. Hampton 4.) Married to Ulysses Doan, at Milton Doan's, Linn Co., Ia., 1856-6-10. They lived first, three miles from Springville, Ia. Moved to Grundy Co., Mo., 1866 (?) Back to Iowa in 1867, and lived in Boone Co. In 1876, went to Rice Co., Kan. Thence in the spring of 1900, to Reno Co., Kan. Here her husband died Nov. 8th, 1900, at Turon, Reno Co., Kan.

He was the second child of Milton and Ruthanna (Slack) Doan and born 1834-6-28, orthodox Friend and a Republican.

Children of Ann P. (Hampton) Doan:

I ISRAEL MILTON DOAN, born 1857-8-21, married 1st, Minnie Jane Hanks, 1877-7-7, she died 1878-4-24, at Sterling, Kansas. Married 2nd, Sophia Doan, his cousin and daughter of Wm. P. and Ann H. Doan, of Muskingum Co., O., at Hutchison, Kan., 1889-9-25.

Children of Israel M. and Sophia Doan:

1. WILLIAM CLARENCE, born 1889-8-15.
2. HARRY MILTON, born 1894-11-19.

II EDMUND BAILEY DOAN, born 1861-5-30. Married Cora B. Pemplin, 1898-5-19. No children.

III ELIZA PIERPONT DOAN, twin to Edmund, married 1st, Albert P. Williams, 1879-3-15. Had two children:

1. MAMIE, born 1881-7-25, and died Oct. 1884.
2. ORA, born Sept., 1887.

Eliza's husband died Sept., 1902. She was married 2nd to Walter Gidley, of Hargroves, Rush Co., Kan., April 1904.

IV ALBERT W. DOAN, born 1863-8-14, and died 1889-4-1, married Mary W. Wire, 1881-12-7.

Children of Albert and Mary W. Doan:

1. CLAUDE VERNON, born 1883-12-26, in Rice Co., Kansas.
2. IRVIE JAMES, born 1885-10-26, in Rice Co., Kan.
3. ADDIE ALICE, born 188- -3-3, at Turon, Rush Co., Kansas.

V SAMUEL HAMPTON DOAN, born 1863-8-14. Twin to Albert and married Dora A. Ballard, 1886-1-20, and died 1889-4-23. No children.

54 ISAAC STEERE (5) HAMPTON, (Samuel 4, John 3, John 2, Joseph 1) born 1841-2-14, in Chesterfield, O. (See Samuel Betts 4) Married 1863-2-12, Elizabeth Ellen Hazelrig, near Viola, Linn Co., Ia., who was born there 1841-10-3, and daughter of Charles and Mary Hazelrig, from Indiana.

Isaac and wife lived in Linn Co., till 1874, when they moved to Rice Co., Kan., in 1878, to Orange Co., Kan., 1886, to San Diego, Cal., and in 1899, to Fresno Co., Cal., where he was in 1907. Religion orthodox Friends. Politics, Prohibitionist. Occupation, farming, stock raising and dairying.

Children:

I CHARLES GRANT, born 1864-2-12, died 1883-11-21, of consumption.

II LUELLA, born 1865-5-26, died 1865-9-16.

III ARTHUR, born 1866-9-27, died 1867-6-13.

99 IV NETTIE, born 1868-6-20.

100 V SAMUEL B., born 1870-2-26.

101 VI IDA, born 1872-11-12.

Above six born in Linn Co., Ia.

102 VII CORA BELLE, born 1876-6-25, at Sterling, Rice Co., Kan.

VIII ETHEL, born 1880-4-1, at Barclay, Orange Co., Kan., died 7-25-1880.

Mary Ellen Hampton, mother of the above eight children died of consumption at Barclay, Kan., 1882-3-25.

On 9th month, 3rd, 1883, Isaac married Elizabeth Plummer Hirst, at Springville, Ia.

Children of Second Marriage:

103 I WILLIAM EVERETT, born 1892-6-6.

II MARY EDITH, twin to Wm. E., died 1895-6-22.

55 RICHARD BETTS (5) HAMPTON, (Samuel B. 4, John 3, John 2, Joseph 1) born 1844-11-2, in Chesterfield, O. (See life of Samuel Betts 4) Married Maria Bailey in 1864.

Children:

104 I CLINTON E., born 1864-10-21.

105 II MARY JANE, born 1866-10-12.

III JESSE B., born 1868-11-4, died 1877-8-28.

IV EVALINDA, born 1871-1-16, married to Edwin E. Dodson and died 1899-6-2.

V ELIZABETH, born 1873-4-18, died 1888-9-13.

106 VI JOSEPH, born 1875-9-3.
107 VII WILLIAM, born 1877-10-13.
108 VIII JOHN P., born 1880-1-16.
109 IX ANNA, born 1882-3-26.
110 X RUTH, born 1884-4-21.

Maria Bailey Hampton, the mother of these children, died 1907-10-8, near Wenatchee, Washington. Buried in Damorris monthly meeting grave yard, near Dwight Kan.

Richard failed to make any satisfactory report of his life or of his family although earnestly solicited. Items were gathered from others.

56

WILLIAM STEERE (5) HAMPTON, (Samuel B. 4, John 3, John 2, Joseph 1) born 1847-2-8, near Pierpoints Mill, Penn Tp., Morgan Co., O., was moved with the family to Linn Co., Ia., in 1851, married Lora A. Branch at Marion, Ia., 1866-4-21.

Children:

I EDWIN DeFOREST, born 1870-2-14, died 1888-5-24, at America, Kan. A Christian young man.
111 II FRANK A., born 1872-12-19.
112 III MAUDE, born 1879-9-3.

After marriage, Wm. S. Hampton and wife lived first at Springville, Ia., 8 years; at Cedar Rapids 10 years; at Americus, Kan., 12 years; at Emporia, Kan., 10 years. (June, 1906.)

In religion, Methodist Episcopal; in politics, Republican. Failed to respond to further repeated inquiries about his life and family.

57

EMILY (5) HAMPTON, (Cary 4, John 3, John 2, Joseph 1) born 1836-4-30, in Guernsey Co., O. Lived in childhood in several places in Ohio and one in Va., as related in the history of her father. Later in Meigs Co., O., Bethany, Va., and Pike Co., O. Here she was married at California (P. O. then Flat, since Stockdale) to Elijah H. Wells, 1854-1-7, a prosperous and religious man of the

United Brethren church.

Children of Emily (Hampton) Wells all born in Pike Co., O.

I WM. SOLOMON WELLS, born 1856-10-15, married Mary Adams, 1876-10-15, at California, Pike Co., O., daughter of Wm. and Sarah Malinda (Bennett) Adams, both natives of Scioto Co., O.

Mary was born Dec. 14th, 1858.

Children of Wm. S. and Mary (Adams) Wells:

1. VERNA ELLIS, born 1877-6-22, died in infancy.
2. JOY ALICE, born 1878-10-17, married 1903, John W. English, of Sterling, Kan., born at Chillicothe, O., and is a retired exchange and land broker.

3 and 4. WILLIAM LLOYD, ELIJAH FLOYD, twins, born 1881-3-3. William Lloyd a barber. Elijah Floyd studying law in 1908.

5. EDGAR ROSS, born 1883-4-19.
6. DAISY PEARL, born 1885-12-3.
7. FLOSSIE MYRTLE, born 1888-9-15.
8. INA VIOLET, born 1893-9-4.

Mr. Wells moved to Sterling, Kan. Had lived at Given Station, O. Had also lived nearly two years, 1874-6, at Norwood, Minn. Occupation Feb. 1908, insurance and real estate agent. Baptist. Democrat.

II MARY ALICE WELLS, born 1858-1-8, married to James Silas Rickey, 1875-2-6, at Stockdale, O.

Children of Mary Alice (Wells) Rickey:

1. LEWIS DENVER RICKEY, born 1876-8-24.
2. CHARLES EDWIN RICKEY, born 1878-8-22.
3. EPHRIAM ELIJAH Rickey, born 1880-12-26.

She was a Christian woman, converted in early life and a member of the Methodist Protestant church. She died 1890-7-26, near Stockdale, (California) O.

III HENRY JONES WELLS, born 1860-4-22, married 1st, Lizzie Parrill, daughter of Anges and Nancy Parrill,

1888-10-28, who died 1895-8-8, born 1865, at Beaver, Pike Co., O.

Married 2nd, Lena M. Rapp, daughter of Christian and Anna Marie Rapp, and born 1869, at Beaver, Pike Co., O.

Children of Henry J. Wells:

1. RAY H., 1894-6-4, by first wife.
2. ELLIS N., born 1897-9-15, by second wife.
3. EMILY V., born 1906.

A farmer, Methodist, Republican. In civil affairs has held office of Township Trustee. In church, Class Leader and Trustee.

IV JOHN D. WELLS, born 1862-8-2, married Mary B. Hallowell, 1888-8-30, at Hutchinson, Kansas.

Children of John D. Wells:

1. CLIFFORD RAY, born 1890-6-11.
2. WINFIELD WILLARD, born 1893-2-8.

John D. Wells is a farmer, an Episcopal Methodist and a Prohibitionist.

V. NATHAN H. WELLS, born 1865-5-28, and died 1865-12-14.

Elijah H. Wells, father of the above five (5) children of Emily, died 1870-5-10. A little over four years after his death Emily married Thomas Kirkpatrick, June 30th, 1874. With him she lived over 25 years. "He was a farmer and prosperous in his business. A Christian man and a member of the Methodist Episcopal church, died 1899-8-13, within a few days of 75 years old.

Child of Emily's Second Marriage:

THOMAS MOODY KIRKPATRICK, born 1881-12-16, at Madison Tp., Scioto Co., O., where his early life was spent. Educated in common school. Married MARIA

McKINLEY, of same Tp., 1901-8-17, born 1883-7-8, at same place. Daughter of Wm. and Rachel (Odle) McKinley, both natives of Scioto Co.

Children of T. Moody Kirkpatrick:

1. DAISY MARIE, born 1902-8-14, in the house where her father was born.

2. IDA MURDITH, born 1904-10-26, at Springdale, Stephens Co., Washington. "Moody Kirk" and wife lived first on the farm where he was born, for two years. In Portsmouth, O., 9-1-1903, to 3-1-1904. Then moved to Washington and lived at Delkena and at Springdale in Stevens Co., and at Spokane. One month at Nelson, British Columbia 8-1 to 9-1-1904, and then to Spokane, Wash., 1905-7, and back again to Springdale, where their home was in 1908. Occupation 1908, woodman and teamster. Episcopal Methodist, Prohibitionists.

Emily's 2nd husband, Thos. Kirkpatrick, died 1899-8-13. After nearly three more years of widowhood, Emily was married to John B. Brown. She reports herself as having lived happily with each of her husbands. Says: "Peace always reigned in our home." Mr. Brown is a farmer and prosperous. "He served three years as a soldier in the War for the Union. He was converted at 13 years and has been a member of the Methodist Protestant church from youth. Is also a steward and a class leader in that church."

Of her children she says: "All were converted in youth," and adds: "In regard to myself I can say in truth I have been trying to live a Christian life from early youth and have been a member of the United Brethren, Methodist Episcopal and Methodist Protestant churches," (going in each case into the church to which her husband belonged,) "and a Sabbath School teacher a good part of the time," "Have a class at the present time (Aug. 6th, 1906) and have only been absent three times in the last 17 months." She died 1910-7-13.

58 SOLOMON ERNEST (5) HAMPTON, (Cary 4, John 3, John 2, Joseph 1) born 1837-9-14. "From 1843 to 1855, most of his time was spent in school, a considerable part of the time being at Bethany, Va.

"In the spring of 1855, he in company with his sister, Asenath, went to Blackhawk Co., Ia., intending to make their home with their sister, Mary and her husband, Daniel G. Ellis.

"In the fall following he went with Samuel Ellis, a cousin of D. G. Ellis, to Minnesota, and made his home with Thom Van Eaton, a brother-in-law of James Hiram Hampton. (Solomon's half brother). During the following winter, he had his fingers, toes, cheeks, and nose badly frozen in a blizzard which struck him and Mr. Van Eaton on their way home with a load of rails on a sled drawn by a yoke of oxen, while crossing a prairie two and one-half miles wide, which lay between the farm of Mr. Van Eaton and a timber lot which the latter owned on the Cannon river, 35 miles southwest of St. Paul."

"Early in the spring of 1856, he went to Goodhue Co., adjoining on the east and "squatted," that is laid claim to a quarter section of land through which ran the Zumbro river, hoping to hold it till the following September, at which time the government had issued orders that all lands not preempted, in this county, should be sold, he being under age, could not preempt it. He was building a hewed log house and had just raised it to the square when a party of gentlemen looking for a town site offered him a price for it which he accepted and immediately returned to Blackhawk Co., Ia., to attend the wedding of his sister, Asenath. He remained with D. G. Ellis, until the fall of 1857, and then taught a public school in that county."

"In the spring of 1858, he went with his brother, Hiram and family, to Neosho Co., Kan., where each bought 'government' land and while Hiram was hauling lumber from Kansas City, distant 100 miles, to build a house, he, Solomon, broke prairie with a two-foot plow and five yoke of oxen which they had purchased in Missouri, as they passed through from Iowa. While their little cousin Jesse Hampton, who came with them "chopped in seed corn."

"In the following fall owing to continued ill health, he returned to Ohio. During the next few years he taught school in the winter and devoted his spare time to the study of medicine."

"In 1862, he visited his father in Jefferson Co., Ind., who was practicing medicine there, and in August of that year he enlisted in the 77th Reg., (4th Cavalry) Ind. Volunteers. On the 2nd, of the following October, he received a gun shot wound in the left shoulder in a skirmish with Gen. Bragg's forces at Mt. Washington, twenty miles south of Louisville, Ky.

"The next day he was sent to Jefferson Co., Ind., on a furlough and made his home with his father.

"He was honorably discharged on account of the disability caused by the wound, the bullet having lodged near the spine and still remaining to date, July 29th, 1909.

"The disability was not such as to disqualify him for teaching school and studying medicine; and he devoted his time industriously to these vocations, attending his first regular course of lectures at the Starling Medical College, of Columbus O., in 1864, and his second at theMiami Medical College, of Cincinnati, O., at which he graduated in Feb., 1866.

"In the summer of 1865, he re-enlisted for guard duty in the 137th Reg., Ind. Vols. "One-hundred days service." In March 1866, he commenced the practice of medicine at Forks of Locust, in Carroll Co., Ky., and at once gained a large patronage as there was a great deal of sickness and no doctor nearer than Carrollton, the county seat, distant six miles. Some of his patrons of 1866, have been under his professional care continuously to the present time. (July, 1909.)

"Through the earnest solicitations of Capt. M. J. Hoagland, George H. Conway and others, he was induced to enter into a partnership with Dr. Harvey A. Moore, a graduate of the Jefferson Medical College, of Philadelphia, Pa., who was and for several years had been in bad health. This partnership continued till Dr. Moore's death in 1868.

"Capt. Hoagland, above mentioned, was the son of Major M. T. Hoagland, who served on Gen. Jackson's staff in the war of 1812, and the Mr. Conway was a son of Mr. Peter Conway and a brother-in-law of Major M. T. Hoagland, two of the most esteemed and influential families in the county, if not in the state.

Dr. H. A. Moore had married two of Major M. T. Hoagland's daughters, each dying within two years after marriage, the second wife leaving an infant daughter, born March 3rd, 1850, named MARY CAROLINE MOORE, whom the subject of this sketch married Dec. 22, 1870, at the home of her grandfather Hoagland, which had also been her home from infancy, in presence of a host of relatives and friends, the groom's best man being the present Chief Chemist of the Department of Agriculture, Dr. Harvey W. Wiley, who had been studying medicine with him for two years.

"In the spring of 1873, owing to continued ill health, Dr. Hampton and wife moved to a farm they had purchased in Hunter's Bottom, claimed to be the grandest spot in Kentucky—six miles above Milton, on the Ohio river, and resigned the greater part of his practice which by this time had become quite extensive as well as lucrative and engaged tenants to cultivate the farm. But before the end of the year his health greatly improved and he resumed and still holds considerable practice.

"In 1868 Dr. Hampton joined the Baptist church at Corn Creek, four miles south of Milton, and as there was no church in Milton, he at once set about building a church edifice with a Masonic hall over it and succeeded beyond his most sanguine expectations. On the 23rd of June, 1870, a church of about forty members was organized and the edifice paid for and solemnly dedicated in the presence of a large concourse of people.

"On the following day the Masonic Hall was duly dedicated by the Grand Master of the Grand Lodge, of

Ky. Dr. Hampton being a member of both institutions, as he is today; and is now a Knight Templar Mason.

"On June 28th, 1909, this Milton Lodge No. 461 F. & A. M., made a record which is said in the annals of Masonry, to be unique. Dr. Hampton in the Masonic Hall which he was principally instrumental in building, nearly forty years ago, was the Worshipful Master; his oldest son, Moses Jackson Hampton, Senior Warden, and his second son, Harvey Moore Hampton, Junior Warden, and his youngest and only remaining son, Walton Lawrence Hampton, was the candidate upon whom the father and two sons conferred the sublime degree of Master Mason, in a thorough and impressive manner, aided by stereoptican illustrations on canvas. In honor of this event the lodge gave a royal banquet to the Hamptons and its members and invited guests.

"Dr. Hampton was editor of the W. C. T. U. column in the Milton News for many years. Is a strong advocate of prohibition. Has lived to see his own town and county "dry" and glories in the progress being now made and hopes to live to see the monster utterly destroyed.

"He was President of the Jefferson Co., Ind., Medical Society, a member of the Indiana State Medical Society, also of the American Medical Association when he assisted in organizing the Carroll Co. Medicio-Chirugical Society, and was its first President. He is also a member of the Kentucky State Medical Society, of the Board of Health of Carroll Co., and also of the Board of Examining Surgeons of the Bureau of Pensions, located at Carrollton, the county seat of Carroll Co.

"Dr. Hampton took an active part in organizing "A. S. of E." and the Burley Tobacco Society in 1906, and was on the committee of the latter at Winchester, that drafted its constitution and by-laws and was the first President of the Carroll Co. Board of Control, the Burley Tobacco Society being composed of the various county Boards of Control.

"After the death of Major M. T. Hoagland, in 1869, and of Capt. M. J. Hoagland, in 1879, there being no male member of the family consisting then only of two maiden daughters of Major Hoagland, Ellen P. and Addie Hoagland, to care for them and the large estate left by their father, Dr. Hampton and family moved into the old home of his wife and are now living there, the aunts being now 90 and 72 years old respectively.

"Dr. Hampton and family are highly esteemed and respected by a host of friends and relatives."

Children:

113 I MARY EMILY, born 1873-5-2.
114 II MOSES JACKSON, born 1875-2-28.
115 III ELLA KATE, born 1877-5-2.
116 IV BESSIE PAYNE, born 1878-12-6.
117 V HARVEY MOORE, born 1880-8-6.
118 VI WALTON LAWRENCE, born 1882-10-7.

59

ASENATH (5) HAMPTON, (Cary 4, John 3, John 2, Joseph 1) born 1840-7-3, at Coles Landing on Ohio river a few miles above Parkersburg, Va., (now W. Va.) was moved with the family to Ohio in her first year and lived in several places as related in Cary's life till after her mother's death in 1850, when she went to live with her aunt, Asenath Doan, in Athens Co., and remained over a year and in 1852, went to live with her father at California, Pike Co., he having married again. After her sister Emily's marriage she lived awhile with her at the same place. Lived a part of a year at Albany, Athens Co., with a family named Bean and went to school part of the time. She also lived with her older half-sister, Mary Ellis, at Waterloo, Blackhawk Co., Ia., going there with her brother, Solomon, in 1855.

Near Waterloo, Iowa, 1856-6-12, married to Solomon Levi Gable, born 1831-2-18, and son of Solomon and Elizabeth (Dull) Gable, of York Co., Penn., where he was born. Was a farmer.

They first lived at Waterloo. Spring of 1857, went to Van Buren Co., spring of 1858, moved to Detroit,

Crawford Co. Her memoir sent by daughter, Ida Alice, says: "They came to Crawford Co., in 1858. First lived in Millford Tp., then in Denison, then in Coon Grove, and finally removed to the homestead in Millford Tp., which was their home for many years. In 1895 rented their farm and moved into Denison. They spent two winters in California."

She died at Denison, July 8th, 1907. The memoir adds: "She was converted in her childhood." (Youth rather). She was active in all departments of Christian work. In Millford township, she was the center of Christian activity of the country side. Superintendent of the Sunday School, President of the Missionary Society, Ladies Aid Society and at the head of all good work. Upon moving to Denison, she took the same active part in church and temperance work.

"While she endeavored to do her whole duty to her fellow men it was in the home that the purity and the strength of her character showed to the fullest. She was an ideal wife and mother."

A local newspaper at Denison, in noticing her death, uses this language: "Mrs. Gable was one of nature's noble women and leaves to her family and friends a heritage all can be proud of forever."

She "was a refined and cultivated lady and in her later years compiled a history of her family which makes a large book well written. In this history, she gives in detail her experience and related tales of hardships and hope which she experienced from the time she first came to Iowa. Few of the present generation will ever know what it is to go through the dark and cloudy days she has and few will have a brighter closing of their lives."

She made a copy of her family history for each child. Her son-in-law, G. P. Hirst, sent extracts from his copy of her history, from which the following items are copied.

Of her life at her Uncle Wm. Doan's, after her mother's death, she says: "My uncle's family were very kind to me and tried to make me feel at home. I soon became reconciled and very happy with them. They lived on a farm surrounded by the grand old woods of Ohio. I was fond of walking through them. There was a great charm for me in their grandeur and solitude. Uncle William was a very cheerful and pleasant old man and his society was much sought after by both young and old. His opinions on moral questions were in advance of the time in which he lived. His sincerity was so evident that he compelled the respect and gained the friendship of many who did not share his opinions."

"While I lived in the family, the question of slavery was being agitated. The principles of freedom and equality before the law, early entered Uncle William's soul and in later years seemed to possess his entire being. For many years he assisted runaway slaves. Some of the experiences of those days are thrilling. He was threatened by slave owners (rather by pro-slavery people in Ohio) for his outspoken opposition to slavery and likely would have been mobbed but for his coolness and courage."

"Speaking of 'Uncle Tom's Cabin,' then being published, in serial form, Mrs. Gable says, further: "From week to week Uncle William would ask me to read the story to him. He would become greatly excited while listening to the author's graphic account of the evils and injustice of slavery. When I read about Eliza crossing the river on the floating ice with her babe in her arms, the slave pens and auction sale of Emiline and other thrilling chapters he would walk the floor with rapid strides, often interrupting me with exclamations of wrath at the monstrous outrages of the slave traffic which, thanks be to God and brave good men, like Uncle William Doan, has become a thing of the past. The battle now is against the rum power and its similar horrors."

"Aunt Asenath fully shared the views of her husband and encouraged him in his advanced theories of reform. She was a model wife and mother with a heart full of love for every living creature. I shall always cherish her memory for her kindness to me when I was a motherless little girl."

"How well I remember her calm, peaceful face

which nothing could disturb. She used the Quaker phraseology and dressed in the style of that sect. She wore a cap of plain fine white goods with a scarf of the same material around her neck and neatly folded over her bosom. Her dress was of some sober color and always scrupulously neat."

"She took a cold water bath every morning and was an enthusiastic advocate of the "cold water cure."

Mrs. Gable says further of her aunt, Asenath: "She was interested in my education and taught me many things not taught in the common schools of that time."

"This dear aunt lived to be nearly 90 years old and her husband died in his 85th year. They were honored and loved by all who knew them except those whose evil practices they so strongly denounced and even these had to respect them for their life of honest endeavor to serve the best interests of humanity."

March 30th, 1906, Mrs. Gable wrote to the compiler of this history, in part, as follows:

"I never went to school much after I left Aunt Asenath's. Have always read a good deal and have picked up a little learning from observation. I joined the Methodist Episcopal Church before I was married and have been a Methodist Episcopal ever since. I have been interested in temperance work ever since I learned the evils of intemperance in your father's house, when a little girl. I have been President of the Woman's Christian Temperance Union for many years, and hope to live to see the overthrow of the rum power.

Sincerely your cousin,

Asenath Gable."

Children of Asenath (Hampton) Gable:

I AMOS BYRON GABLE, born 1857-4-10, in Blackhawk Co., Ia. Married Josephine Beach, 1878-10-8, at Tipton, Cedar Co., Ia., daughter of Marcus and Cornelia Beach, of Tipton. Her proper name was Josephine and she was so baptized, but in her youth she was called "Feney" and she sometimes so wrote it. By an error of someone it is "Feney" on the license record of Cedar Co., but it should be Josephine.

They lived at Tipton, after marriage, 1879. Ten years later moved to Hartington, Neb. His occupation has been somewhat varied. For 18 years prior to report, Feb. 1908, it was dealing in live stock and real estate.

Episcopalian. Republican.

Mayor of city of Hartington many years.

Children of A. B. Gable:

I. LOIS C., born 1880-3-20, married to Herman P. Rankin, 1900-3-20. Reside at Hartington, Neb.

Children of Lois C.

1. MARTIN, born 1904-6-8.
2. CORNELIA, born 1905-10-9.
3. JAMES LEE, born 1907-7-8.

2. OLGA, born 1883-7-24, married to J. Lee Prince, 1905-7-19. Reside at Hartington, Neb.

Children of Olga:

1. IRENE, born 1906-8-20.
2. JAY LEE, born 1907-10-24.

3. EDNA, born 1886-5-13.
4. HAZEL, born 1892-2- and died 1892-9-28.

II IDA ALICE GABLE, born 1859-3-19, at Detroit, Crawford Co., Ia. Married to Cyrus Greek at the home of her parents at Vail, Crawford Co., Ia., 1878-12-31. He was the son of Sylvanus Benjamin and Lucina (Goodrich) Greek, of Denison, Ia.

Ida and her husband lived first after marriage at Denison, three years, then at Mapleton, Ia., 8 years, at Omaha, Neb., three years and at Genoa, Neb., 15 years, prior to report Feb. 9th, 1908.

Husband's occupation: Dealer in real estate and live stock.

She took a lively interest in the preparation of this history and wrote encouragingly about it. Was the first to offer financial aid and the first to send it.

In speaking of her early life "in a wild country," and the lack of such advantages of school as children of today have, she refers very tenderly to the hardships and privations her parents endured in those early days and in a Christian and philosophic spirit, says: "Those hardships and privations that my parents endured in my early childhood are not dark spots in my memory, but on the contrary are bright recollections; and then refers to the pleasure she has in having her aged father with her and in listening to him relate on winter evenings, the story of those early days.

Congregational in church fellowship.

Children of Ida Alice:

1. LESLIE ALBIN GREEK, born 1879-10-14, married Lena Smoleski, 1907-2-24. A farmer at Fullerton, Neb. (Feb. 1908.)

2. ETHEL ASENATH GREEK, born 1881-4-19, married to Harry Peter Hansen, 1903-4-19. A farmer at Anoka, Boyd Co., Neb. (Feb. 1908.)

3. MAURICE CYRUS GREEK, born 1884-1-10, married Hattie Blanch Parkerson, 1905-1-28. A farmer at Fullerton, Neb. (Feb. 1908).

4. ZELA MYRTLE GREEK, born 1887-3-5, died 1890-11-25.

5. ALICE LEE GREEK, born 1892-1-22. Attending school at home. (Feb. 1908.)

6. VERNA BERNICE GREEK, born 1896-11-10.

III GEORGE HARVEY GABLE, born 1860-11-11. Graduated from the law department of the Michigan University, at Ann Arbor, in the spring of 1888. Then worked at common labor until he earned money enough to start practice.

"He began practice at Council Bluffs, Ia., in the spring of 1899. Married Ida Germain at Logan, Ia., 1896-7-2. Her father was a Methodist minister. Her mother died when Ida was about 15 years old. Child, Norvin, born 1899-8-9. (Norvin's father wrote that he was 8 years old, Oct. 8th, 1907. But his Uncle Mearl, gives his birth Aug. 9th, 1899.) Living with uncle Mearl at last report.

Mr. Gable has gained quite a reputation as a public speaker in Iowa. Has served three years in a minor civil office. Held several positions at the head of local societies at Council Bluffs. Was Deputy Grand Master of the A. O. W. U., at date of report, Feb. 1908. Died 1909-6-15, as result of a fall on icy pavement some months before. Buried at Denison, Ia.

IV MARY EMILY GABLE, born 1863-1-15, near Vail, Crawford Co., Ia., and lived there with her parents, till 18 years of age, when she went to live with her uncles, the Gable brothers at Woodland, Cal. From there she attended the seminary at Bornicia and except one or two visits to her parents, remained with them till her marriage to GRANVILLE PERCY HURST, 1889-2-6, at Sacramento, Cal.

"She was of beautiful form and person and a favorite in social circles where she moved, but she voluntarily gave up what is commonly called society and devoted her time to her home and family."

"Later she took up the work of the Woman's Christian Temperance Union and was soon regarded as a leader in the organization in the county and city where she lived.

"Her interest in and love for children was early recognized by her co-workers and she was elected County Superintendent of Mother's Work, which position she held at her death.

"She was also superintendent of the local organization in her home city and was such when the end came.

"Her death was deplored by old and young and at a meeting of the W. C. T. U. to arrange to attend the funeral in a body, the whole assembly were in tears and many members sobbed like children.

"Mrs Hurst was an intense lover of the beautiful. The sky jeweled with stars or gilded with light, or varigated with clouds all filled her soul with the exalted pleasure that only poets and artists feel. And she was as fully alive to moral beauty. Every virtue or exalted quality of the heart and mind touched a responsive chord in her being. Taken all in all she was one of God's noblest women and was loved and prized through the wide circle of her acquaintances.

"Her love of nature found expression in pictures. Pictures in oil and crayon are among the souvenirs most cherished by her family.

"Her two daughters have inherited her love for art and nature; and the older, Veta, possesses a talent in that direction which amounts to genius and she will make art her life work."

At the time of her death, a highly appreciative notice of over a column's length, appeared in the "Home Alliance," a local paper of Woodland.

A memoir (The memoir was written by Emily Hoppin, State Treasurer of the W. C. T. U., of California) also appeared in the "Pacific Ensign," of San Francisco, closing with the following lines, taken from a poem by Mrs. H. A. Merritt, on the occasion of Mrs. Hurst's death:

"With friends a cordon round
With sympathies encircling all the world
How sweet to stay—how sweet to go
A most propitious moment to go hence.

"Now who will wear the purple or open wide
Her door to all, show warmest friendship
Living to bless each moment as it comes
To reach out hands of blessing everywhere."

She died August 14th, 1901. Was a Methodist, but liberal and tolerate of other's views.

Her husband, born 1851-10-7, near Milon, Missouri, was the son of William and Elmina (Sigler) Hurst. The father, a native of West Va., and the mother of Cumberland, Md.

Occupation, law; politics, formerly Republican but for 20 years afterward, Prohibitionist. Says: "My religion is to do good. Do not belong to any church but help to support several. I have at all times since 18 years of age, fought the liquor traffic and will fight it till I die or the saloons are gone.

"It may seem like a boast but it has been an ambition with me to show that a lawyer can be an honest man, need not be a liar nor the champion of wrong for hire or otherwise. How far I have succeeded, ask my neighbors and the business men of Woodland."

Children of Mary Emily:

1. VETA LEOLA HURST, born 1889-11-28, Thanksgiving Day at Woodland, Cal. "Is a natural artist and will enter an art school at San Francisco, next year." (March 20th, 1908.)
2. PERCIE ASENATH HURST, born at Woodland, Cal., 1894-7-18.

"She has her mother's sweet placid nature and also her artistic temperament. That she is so like her mother is one of the blessed things in my life." (Their father's letter.)

These two girls are our only children and comprise my family since their mother's death." (G.H.P., Mar. 20th, 1908.)

V WALTER HAMPTON GABLE, born 1866-2-7, in Crawford Co., Ia. Lived there and at Milton, Ky., Cincinnati, O., Tripp, S. D., and at Plainview, Neb., previous to marriage. Educated at Vail, Ia., and Hanover, Ind. Married Nelly Forbes, 1895-3-14, at Westside, Ia., born

1874-5-17, at Marshaltown, Ia., and daughter of Nathan S. and Jane (Drane) Forbes. Father of Scotch descent and born in Ill. Mother of Irish descent and born in Iowa.

After marriage, Walter and wife lived on a farm near Denison, Iowa, and later on one near Plainview, Nebraska. Farmer, stock raiser and dealer. Congregationalist, Republican. Has been township clerk, member of school board and Sunday school superintendent.

Wife a Methodist, has been superintendent of Sunday School and Secretary of Epworth League.

Children of Walter H.

1. HAROLD HAMPTON GABLE, born 1898-4-4, near Denison, Ia.
2. HARMON LEVI GABLE, born 1902-6-16, near Plainview, Neb.
3. ARTHUR MEARL GABLE, born 1906-9-5, near Plainview, Neb.

VI LEWIS MARTIN GABLE, born 1868-5-30, in Crawford Co., Ia. Graduated from the Law Department of the Iowa State University, June 12th, 1895. Located at Genoa, Neb., and commenced the practice of law. Went to Wagner, S. D., March 28th, 1902, and engaged in the practice of law and dealing in real estate.

Married 1902-3-27, at Genoa, Neb., Myrtle Slaughter, daughter of Peter and Margaret (Hayes) Slaughter and born 1878-3-11, at Emerson, Mills Co., Ia. Her parents were born at Athens, Missouri, but their parents came from Virginia and Kentucky.

He is a Methodist and a Republican.

Child: Edgar Slaughter, born 1905-11-1.

VII EFFIE MYRTLE GABLE, born 1870-4-9. "The joy of our lives for nineteen years," her mother wrote. Died 1899-7-27.

VIII SOLOMON LEVI GABLE, born 1872-3-4. Educated in common schools and a short time in Cornell College, Mt. Vernon, Ia., in 1891-2. Married at Denison, Ia., 1901-12-25, Minnie Tower, daughter of Salem and Agnes (Calderwood) Tower, and born 1875-11-2, in Crawford Co., Ia. Father born in Whiteside Co., Ill., and mother in Scotland.

In January, 1902, shortly after marriage, Mr. Gable and his bride, went to Wagner, S. D., where their home has been to date of report, Feb. 1908. In 1905 and 1906, he was deputy treasurer of Charles Mix Co. In 1908, City Treasurer of Wagner. Episcopal Methodist. Republican. Occupation, Feb. 1908, Assistant Bank Cashier.

Child of Solomon Levi Gable:

1. RUTH AGNES GABLE, born 1903-3-9.

IX EDWARD ELERY GABLE, born 1874, in Crawford Co., Ia. Educated first in country schools in winter, then a three years course in Denison High School. Went to Plainview, Neb., in 1897. Moved to Oakton, Neb., in 1906, and engaged in dealing in real estate. Methodist. Republican. Unmarried at date of report, March 6th, 1908.

X MEARL ARTHUR GABLE, born 1878-12-23, in Millford Tp., Crawford Co., Ia., and lived there on a farm in early life and later in Denison, same county. Education began in county district school. Graduated from Denison High School and then from Denison Normal School. In June, 1905, graduated from Simpson College, Indianola, Ia.

Licensed to preach fall of 1904: Appointed to Panama, Ia., in Des Moines conference,in fall of 1905 and Defiance, in fall of 1906. Admitted to DesMoines Conference, on trial, in September, 1907. Entered Garret Bibical Institute at Everston, Ill., the same month and appointed to serve New Buffalo, Mich., as preacher in addition to school work. Left in June, 1909, with one more year's work to do which he expected to return in fall of 1910, and perform. Married 1905-5-19, ETHELYN LEOTA McKIE, at Three Oaks, Mich., daughter of Edward Hill and Martha Ellen (Mann) McKie and born 1887-6-28. Father a native of Scotland and mother of Indiana.

Ethelyn graduated from Three Oaks High School in 1907. Attended Michigan State Normal School in 1908, and taught a school the same year. She is a member of the Methodist Episcopal Church and president of the local Woman's Foreign Missionary Society, at Lewis, Cass Co., Ia., where her husband is pastor, 1909-10.

XI CHARLES HUGH GABLE, born 1883-10-24. At the age of 7 started to country school. At the age of 12 started to graded school in Denison, Ia., graduated there in 1901. Went to Nebraska State University in the fall of 1904. Began to learn electricial engineering but changed to general science, specializing in entomology. Wrote March, 1908: "Have been out one year but expect to graduate in spring of 1909." Was then a member of the 2nd Presbyterian Church, of Lincoln, Neb., and especially interested in young people. Unmarried.

60

MAHALAH MELVINA (5) HAMPTON, (Cary 4, John 2, Joseph 1) born in Ohio. She was Cary's youngest child and the only one by his second wife, Sarah (Davis) Hampton.

Married a man named Walters, and the last heard from, she was living near New Albany, Ind.

Her half-brother, Solomon, says: "I believe she died in 1876."

Fifth Generation.

NOT OF THE HAMPTON SURNAME.

Only two of the daughters of John (3) Hampton, of Wrightstown, had children, Asenath and Mary Ann. Asenath married William Doan.

Children:

I JOHN HAMPTON DOAN, born 1828-12-10, in Bristol Tp., Morgan Co., O. Had never seen a school house till nearly eight years old, but after that attended about four terms and one month of Friend's schools in two and one-half years, at Chesterfield, Athens Co., O., where the family had moved in the fall of 1836. Moved again with the family, May 15th, 1839, about 20 miles and into Troy Tp., Athens Co. Because of the great distance to school and the need of his help on the farm, only had four terms of school, some of them not full terms, and a few lessons in a geography school in the next seven years.

Read a good deal and studied some at home. In the fall of 1846, walked one term, two and one-half miles to a select school of academic grade at Coolville, same county. Then walked 45 miles and engaged to teach a school for six months near Lytlesburg, in Muskingum Co., for $12 a month of 26 days each. Began teaching Dec. 7th, 1846, three days before 18 years of age. Had taught a geography school of evenings in the summer of 1843.

For three years following the school at Lytlesburg, worked on the farm in spring and summer, attended academic schools in fall and taught in winter. The only exception to this being a trip to Iowa, in spring of 1848, with a lot of fruit trees.

1850-9-15, married Lucetta Webster, of Savannah, (Guysville) Athens Co., O., daughter of Daniel B. and Lois (Stewart) Webster. Went in November following to Canal-Winchester, O., to teach the village school with his young wife as assistant. School a heavy charge. Ninety present one day in one room and of all grades from a-b-c-darians to a pupil in algebra.

Wife's health failed so before spring that she asked to be taken back to her father's which was done. She died March 20th, 1851. A Christian young woman with a taste for intellectual pursuits and a teacher of decided ability.

In spring of 1851, went to school at the Ohio Wesleyan University at Delaware, O., but returned in the summer to Canal Winchester, to teach a select school. Taught a district school in Pickaway Co., O., in the winter and returned to college again in the spring. Went in fall of 1853, to South Charleston, Clarke Co., O., to superintend and teach in the Union Schools there.

Aug. 20th, 1854, married Mary Jeannette Reed, daughter of John and Nancy Ann (Marshall) Reed who were from the eastern shore of Maryland, about Snow Hill.

She was born near South Charleston, 1833-7-27. Her grandmother Reed's maiden name was Jeanette Olivere (Ol-i-ve-re) in English, Oliver, of French family and probably of Heuguenot stock. Her grandmother Marshall's maiden name was Zippora Purnel and of Scotch family. Her grandfather Marshall's Christian name was William Alan.

She had lived several years with her parents in Henry Co., Ia., where her father died. Later she returned to South Charleston and lived with an aunt. Also had lived with an aunt in Philadelphia.

In August, 1855, he became principal of the Ohio Conference Seminary, at Coolville, Athens Co., and continued till the spring of 1859, when he was elected Supt., of Athens Union Schools and served two years and one term.

In the fall of 1861, became principal of Amesville Academy, same county, for one year, and in August, 1862, of Beverly College, Washington Co., four (4) years and one term retiring in November, 1866.

He had joined the Methodist Episcopal Church, at Canal Winchester, in December, 1850, and been converted and after leaving college became active in church work at South Charleston, where he was licensed to exhort in winter of 1854, and was Sunday School Teacher and Class Leader. Licensed to preach at Coolville, in 1856.

In March, 1866, was appointed as junior preacher to supply Sharon circuit, having eight churches located from 9 to 20 miles from Beverly. There he was to serve in connection with his work in the academy for two terms and them give all his time to the churches. March, 1867, admitted to the Pittsburg Conference on trial and sent to Lebanon Circuit with parsonage four and one-half miles from Marietta, one year.

Summerfield three years. Newport two, Deersville one, New Athens spring of 1874, to fall of 1876, counted three years.

That year the old Pittsburg Conference was divided, the Ohio portion becoming a part of the East Ohio. In that portion his lot fell and he was sent to Coldwell one year. Newport again three, Brownsville one, (New Matamoras) Beallsville two. Health failing in 1886, ceased regular work in the ministry.

Went to St. Mary's W. Va., where his oldest son was engaged in the tinning business, put a little capital into it and at the son's request, took charge, manufacturing tinware and doing roofing. Added stove selling and later gasfitting (or plumbing for gas). Retired in fall of 1903.

After going to St. Mary's he did nearly three years missionary work in the Belmont and Waverly Mission. In 1887-8 edited a temperance column in the "St. Mary's Oracle" (newspaper) during the campaign for an amendment to the state constitution prohibiting the liquor traffic.

In the summer of 1888, taught a Normal School at St. Marys. Had assisted in two such schools, one at Coldwell, in 1877, and one at New Matamoras, in 1884. Has continued to take a deep interest in education, visiting schools and attending teacher's institutes as opportunity offered. Has written a good many articles for newspapers, chiefly on moral and educational subjects.

While in the pastorate he introduced the use of Sunday School Institutes as a means of improving the schools in the region where he labored. Also introduced the observance of Children's Day in several places.

Had the reputation of excelling as a reader of hymns in public and as a leader of public prayer for which latter service he was often called upon in various kinds of meetings for many years.

Always cultivated and enjoyed pleasant relations with pastors and people of other denominations.

It fell to his lot to marry a good many people. While in the effective ministry he had 95 weddings recorded and remembered and 251 after going to St. Marys. In all at least 346.

Had a taste for the cultivation of the soil and of plants. Delighted in a good garden. Cultivated one in his eightieth year, mostly with his own hands. Wrote this history without glasses, except the occasional use of a lens to decipher obscure words or numbers, after he was seventy-six and furnished some material for a revised edition of the "Doan Family" history. Had begun collecting items as early as 1865. Espoused the temperance cause in his boyhood and was credited with doing successful work in it, in many places, especially at Newport, Deersville and St. Marys. Sometimes persecuted for activity therein. In 1904, with wife spent over eight months at Cooperstown, N. Y., with son, John K. Doan and family. In like manner spent part of two winters, 1907 and 1909, with son, Edward, at West Carrollton, Montgomery Co., O. April 16th, 1909, moved to latter place.

Children of John H. and M. Jeanette Doan:

I ADDO DOAN, born 1856-7-29. First named Adoniram Judson Doan. His education began in early childhood in his parents' home and was continued in his father's academy and in public schools where he pursued both the common branches and some of academic grade.

Learned the tinner's trade at New Athens, O., in a short apprenticeship, soon becoming expert. Followed the business for several years. Then took up gas-fitting and plumbing, soon coming to be considered a superior mechanic in any branch he attempted to learn.

Near Newport, O., 1877-10-4, married Diantha Allen, daughter of Ira and Diantha (McAlister) Allen. She was born near Marietta, O., 1857-5-8. She joined the Methodist church in youth and became an active member. Was a successful Sabbath School teacher for several years. Was a member of ladies' Societies and of the board of stewards in which latter office she so excelled that she was re-elected several years after asking to be released. A decendent of Ethan Allen, of Revolutionary fame. She had an uncle named Ethan.

Began business at Summerfield, O., in 1876. Moved to Caldwell in 1877, to St. Marys, W. Va., in 1881, and to West Carrollton, O., in 1909. Has always had a taste for reading and in this way has gathered quite a fund of general knowledge.

Was much in demand for a good many years as secretary of meetings or as clerk or judge of elections. Took a leading part in building a church at St. Marys, in 1885. Was trustee, steward and recording steward for a good many years, district steward for several years and conference steward twice. A very efficient worker in Sunday School for several years.

Was a leading member in the Junior Order of American Mechanics during the existence of a council in the place and later in the Tribe of Ben Hur. Deputy Sheriff of Pleasants Co., at one time.

He was a member of the Republican Central Committee of Pleasants Co., W. Va., and secretary of that committee the year the party secured control of the county doing an amount of work no other one equaled. An efficient member of a cornet band for many years.

Was naturally a lover of horses and while yet a boy in his teens, became quite expert at handling a team. Methodist, Republican, but independent.

Children of Addo Doan:

1. HARRY ALLEN, born 1878-7-24, in Coldwell, O. After going to common school and learning to set type in a newspaper office at St. Marys, W. Va., whither the family had moved in his childhood, he was selected by the county superintendent of schools, as a suitable student to represent the county in the corps of military cadets in the State University at Morgantown. Attended two years in 1895 and 1896. He was able to pass over the required course in Mechanic Arts in a few lessons because of his experience in boyhood in his father's tin shop. Could not finish the University course for want of means. He went two seasons with a corps of U. S. Engineers surveying the Ohio river for the purpose of selecting sites for dams and locks to promote navigation. He showed such proficiency and adaptation that he was given charge of a theodolite the second season and when the commander was sick was given charge of the daily reports of the work. He had quite a varied experience, having been assistant tinner, printer, steamboat clerk and assistant pilot, teamster, electrician in an iron mill and is now (1909) an electrician in Wheeling, W. Va., in charge of a squad of workmen.

Married Almina Louisa Gould, a Wheeling school teacher, 1903-12-25. Her father was Pierson Star Gould, born 1838-7-24, in Toronto, Canada, and son of Joseph Herbert Gould and wife both of Pennsylvania. Her mother was Louisa Trask (Doan) Gould, born in Wisconsin, in 1835-2-17, and was daughter of Joshua Doan and wife, Rachel (Hayden) Doan, both of Maine.

Children of Harry A. Doan:

1. HARRY GOULD DOAN, born 1904-10-14, died 1905-6-21.

2. RICHARD STAR DOAN, born 1905-11-12.
3. ALLEN JUDSON DOAN, born 1907-6-27.
4. JOHN REED DOAN, born 1909-1-16.
5. RACHEL JEANETTE DOAN, born 1910-12-10.
Methodist Episcopalian, Republican.

2. FREDERICK TOWNSEND DOAN, born 1882-10-23, at St. Marys, W. Va., on the Ohio river. He seemed to have an innate love of learning. Was anxious to go to school before of legal age. Had to begin his first term near a month late and it was further shortened by sickness at the end, yet he passed through the first and second readers. Was early put to studying music, at home. Then went to Marietta, O., 17 miles away, twice a week for his lessons. He was still so small that a steamboat carried him back and forth without charge.

When not quite fourteen years of age, he entered the Newport High School, a mile away and on the Ohio side of the river about a month after the school year began. Before the first term ended he was advanced to a class that had begun Latin a year before so that finished a four year's course in a little less than three years, having the first honor of his class at graduation. Later he graduated from a business college, at Parkersburg, W. Va. Became stenographer in the U. S. District Attorney's Office there and on quitting that service received a certificate from Judge Blizzard, the attorney, commending him to any who might need his services in which he stated that Fred had been in his employ nearly two years and that if he had any bad habits, he did not know what they were. Not long after, in March, 1905, he was employed by the State Treasurer, of W. Va., in his office at Charleston, the capital. He is now (Oct., 1909) serving his fifth year there.

When at Parkersburg, he continued his musical studies and came to excell greatly as pianist and pipe organist. Episcopalian, Republican.

3. WILLIAM ROE DOAN, born 1891-12-2, at St. Marys, W. Va. An attack of scarlet fever in his seventh

year left him in a partially enfeebled condition and very susceptible to attacks of temporary illness which greatly interfered with his education for several years. He early showed a disposition to earn money for the support of himself and of the family. Was so faithful as an errand boy or a clerk that he could always have a place if anyone could. At 13 years was appointed page of the circuit court and won the good will of the judge and attorneys in a high degree.

Assisted an undertaker for a year or two and soon became able to trim a casket or prepare corpse for burial.

Went with the family to West Carrollton, O., in the spring of 1909, Worked in an automobile repair shop in Dayton, five or six weeks and then took charge of a car for the summer of 1909. Learning machine work with a motor car company, in Dayton, O., 1910.

4 HENRY HOUSTON DOAN, born 1858-10-24, at Coolville, Athens Co., Ohio. Was an enterprising child making plans for the future beyond what might have been expected at his age. Learned to set type in an amateur printing office in his 15th year and same time doing such mechanical work as repairing sewing machines.

In his 16th year he became a student in New Athens College, Harrison Co., O., but could not continue because of poor health. He then persuaded his father to get him a small printing press and let him do job printing. In this he was very successful doing beautiful work which was much admired.

His health grew worse and he sold his printing outfit and went to western Iowa, hoping to improve his health, and worked for several months in a printing office at Glenwood, Mills Co., Ia. Traveled a while for a firm in Chicago, that manufactured stereotype plates for newspapers and worked in an office there and in one in the coppermine region of Lake Superior. Came home to his parents at Caldwell, O., in winter of 1878, with health improved.

Engaged in a tin and stove shop with his brother for a while. Went to railroading but a terrible accident warned him to quit. Worked on a farm, then in Columbus, O., in a stove foundry and with the Columbus Buggy Co., and finally began work in life insurance business but was attacked with fever and died Dec. 23rd, 1884.

He made friends where ever he lived from childhood up and his parents when visiting him on his deathbed were surprised to find how many and how warm his friends were.

A fine singer from a little child and his services in song were much in demand. He was an official member of the Town Street Methodist Church, having been made a steward in six weeks after becoming a full member.

3. WILIAM REED DOAN, born 1861-10-9, and died 1863-5-24.

4. FRANK ISRAEL DOAN, born 1863-9-23, and died 1865-7-17.

5. JOHN KNOWLES DOAN, born 1865-7-27, at Beverly College, O. Early made rapid progress in school and in his 20th year received a certificate to teach in two counties in Ohio and taught a school at Weege, in Belmont Co.

Went to the Ohio Wesleyan University, April 11th, 1887, and finished a six years' course in five years and one term. By hard work as steward of a club and in other ways earned his board most of the time and maintained his standing in his classes. Took great interest in the military department of the college and won in five military contests in four years. This brought him to the head of the battalion of college cadets with rank of Major. He justified himself in giving time and labor to military training in college life on two grounds:

First. Physical exercise and development.

Second. The cultivation of the faculty of attention which lies at the foundation of all learning.

He graduated in the full classical course in June, 1892, and went to Elyria, O., as general secretary of the Young Men's Christian Association. Married Susie May Bentley, 1892-12-8, at Lacrosse, Wisconsin, daughter of Edwin Edward and Susan Nevin (Shepard) Bentley and born 1870-9-21, at Lacrosse. Father born at Gallupville, N. Y., and mother at Nashua, N: H. After preparing for college at Lacrosse, she entered the Ohio Wesleyan University in 1888, and graduated in the full classical course in June, 1892. Her musical education has enabled her to be very helpful to her husband in his Y. M. C. A. work and also in the church where she is a member. She is an active member of the order of The Daughters of the American Revolution.

He resigned at Elyria and went to Denver, Colo., for the sake of his wife's health in the spring of 1893, and worked in a law and commercial reporter's office. In October went to Lincoln, Neb., as General Secretary of the Y. M. C. A., there.

Found scarcely 200 members on October 20th, and led in a campaign for an increase which resulted in an enrollment of 1,000 on March 7th, following, and of 1,125 in November, when he left.

While at Lincoln, he had received two calls to the Utica, N. Y., Y. M. C. A., the second of which he accepted. The Utica association greatly prospered and he remained there about six and a half years, going to Cooperstown, N. Y., as General Secretary, there, in the spring of 1900. While at Utica, he was elected to the same office in the Cincinnati, O., Y. M. C. A., but every member of the Board of Directors at Utica, urged him to stay there and he declined the call to Cincinnati.

Children of John K. Doan and Wife:

1. DOROTHY, born 1894-3-14, died 1909-1-21.
2. DONALD BENTLEY, born 1895-3-21.
3. RUTH, born 1899-3-1.

Both John K. and wife were reared in Methodist

families but are now Presbyterians. Independent Republican.

6 EDWARD BROWN DOAN, born 1869-1-3, in Monroe Co., O. After leaving common school he went a while to the Ohio Wesleyan and then to the Northern University, at Ada, O. Going west he attended the Nebraska State University nearly a year, then one year at Cotner Medical College, near Lincoln Neb. The other three years of his medical course were spent at the Cleveland Homeopathic Medical College, where he graduated April 4th, 1899. He had done five years hard work to get his diploma, working in vacation and one whole year in the time to earn money to pay expenses.

He opened an office, July 12th, 1899, at West Carrollton, Montgomery Co., O., eight miles below Dayton, in the Miama Valley and had a fair practice from the start and at date (1909) has a good practice.

He became interested in the Young Men's Christian Association work while in school and led in the organization of an association in the medical college.

In the annual of the college for 1899, his likeness appears four times, once as member of the graduating class, once as treasurer of the literary society, once as member of the Zeta Chapter of the Phi Alpha Gamma Fraternity, and once as president of the college Y. M. C. A. Became a "church worker" while in school and has been an efficient helper in church affairs since.

After going to West Carrollton, started an agitation against saloons which resulted in driving them out of the township except those inside of an incorporation, to the very great relief of the community.

Married 1903-10-27, Amy Isabel Newell, daughter of Henry L. and Isabel (Macauly) Newell and born at Springfield, Mass., 1884-2-18. Educated in Dayton High School and at Western College for Women at Oxford, O. Both are active members of the Methodist church. She is especially interested in missions and has been a helpful member of both the home and foreign woman's missionary societies.

He is an independent Republican.

Children of Edward B. Doan and Wife:

1. EDWARD NEWELL DOAN, born 1904-10-8.
2. ROSCIUS, born 1906-4-9.
3. JOHN HENRY, born 1907-9-3.
4. RUPERT GADDIS, born 1910-10-18.

7 ROBERT DOAN, born 1873-8-28, and died 1873-10-3.

Mary Jeannette (Reed) Doan, the mother of the foregoing seven sons of John H. Doan, greatly excelled in the number of things needed about a home that she could do and do them well. From weaving a rag carpet to fine needle work and fine knitting, there was scarcely anything she has not done and done well.

Besides cooking and other ordinary duties of a household, she cut and made her little boys' clothes, making her own patterns in the days before patterns were kept in the stores and ready-made clothes for children were not offered or were rare or poor. Excelled in the speed as well as in the quality of her work.

She was awarded a premium for the best specimen of home spun stocking yarn at a county fair at Marrietta, Ohio. It was fully equal to the best factory yarn.

A Methodist and a church goer from her youth up. She taught her children religiously and so arranged her household affairs as to make room for family worship which she conducted herself when her husband was abroad.

She learned fancy (or Indian) basketry after she was seventy and produced beautiful specimens. At seventy-five was still making quilts of extra quality and beauty. Was very provident as well as economical always forecasting the wants of the coming season.

Was a very successful cultivator of flowers and foliage plants and was considered an authority on floriculture in her neighborhood. She took a lively interest in the things that interested her sons, whether work or play, and thus retained their sympathy and confidence and her influence over them for good.

II MARY DOAN, born 1830-9-3, in Bristol Tp., Morgan Co., O., and lived in early life with the family as related in the life of her mother, Asenath Hampton Doan.

Received a common school education and a few terms at a select school in Coolville, O. Taught a term of school in Troy Tp., same county. Married to TITUS SHOTWELL, 1852-10-20, son of Isaac and Hope (Stanton) Shotwell.

They both had a "birth right" membership among the Friends but were "disowned" for being married by a Justice of the Peace, instead of in church which would have required a ride over country roads a distance of about 25 miles and back again twice or 100 miles in all.

He was a farmer and a carpenter. Politically a Republican. They lived first near Little Hocking, in Belpre Tp., Washington Co., O., but about 1855, moved to Troy Tp., Athens Co., near Coolville, onto a small farm joining her father's. About 10 years later moved to Big Run, Rome Tp., but in 18 months returned to their home.

In March, 1880, moved into the Doan homestead to take care of her parents. Here Titus died 1896-1-18, and Mary has continued to make her home. Since her husband's death she has shown good judgment in managing her farm.

Children of Mary D. Shotwell:

1. EVA JANE SHOTWELL, born 1853, died ———
2. ELIAS WHITTIER SHOTWELL, born 1854-10-16, in Washington Co., O. Educated in common school. Worked as a farm hand several years in Ohio. Went to Iowa, April, 1882, to Seneca, Kan., Jan., 1883, and to Osborn, Kan., next spring. Married ANNIE MOORE 1890-11-25, at Osborn, Kan., born in Gage Co., Neb. Her father,

Franklin Moore was born in Scotland, and was a soldier in the civil war nearly 4 years and her mother, Olive (Thornbury) Moore, was born in Ind. His location was, on Jan. 15, 1909, "15 miles from Osborn and about the same from Laray, and about two miles from a direct line between them. Has 160 acres of land, a six-room house and plenty of good out buildings except a barn." Has free rural mail delivery but it is one mile from house. School house two miles away but the children had never been tardy. "Is on school land on the Blue Hills, but has some level land. 20 acres of good alfalfa land.

In politics, he says: "I am a socialist crank—undesirable citizen."

Children of Whittier Shotwell:

1. VELMA HOPE, born 1898-6-9.

2. VERNA MAY, born 1899-11-30.

.Both born at Twin Creek, Kan.

3. ENOS SUMNER SHOTWELL, born 1856-9-16. Educated in common schools. Worked as a farm hand for a while in Muskingum Co., O., where he married ROSE ELTHA MITCHEL, daughter of John and Martha (McClure) Mitchel, 1881-1-, at Zanesville. Continued to live in Meigs Tp., until April 1907, when he moved to Springfield Tp., three and one-half miles west from Zanesville. Methodist and a Republican.

Children of E. Sumner Shotwell:

1. GERTIE, born 1881-5-10. Taught school in Muskingum and in Washington counties. Married to James B. Allison, 1902-5-28. In Nov. 1909, they had four children, 3 boys and 1 girl.

2. GEORGIE, born 1883-9-15. Married to W. C. Blacklege, 1903-11-14. In Nov., 1909, they had two children, both boys.

4 WILLIAM ELERY SHOTWELL, born 1858-10-19. Common school education. Raised on a farm. Went to Perry, Iowa, about 1882. Afterward to Sioux Falls, S. Dakota. Married Minnie Benard. Her parents from Germany.

A carpenter. Poor health.

Children of Wm. E. Shotwell:

I. ELTA, born ———, died June, 1906.
2. EMMA SADIE, born ————?
3. TITUS, born 1894-12-1.
4. THOMAS, born 1896-10-30.
5. WILLIAM, born 1900-6-25.
6. JOHN ———

Failed to answer questions. Items received from sisters.

5 EMILY ANN SHOTWELL, born 1860-9-17. Had common school education. Married to JOHN ELLIOTT MOORE, 1880-11-4, son of Ezekiel and Margaret (Eliott) Moore and born in Washington Co., O., 1864-7-29. Father thought to have been a native of eastern Pennsylvania. Mother born at Steubenville, O.

John E. Moore, died 1888-1-25. Emily with her two children returned to her father's house, after whose death in 1896, she helped her mother not only in household affairs but to manage the farm. Then after seventeen and one-half years of widowhood, she married 2nd ADDISON HAIGHT DEEM, 1905-9-20, and moved to Parkersburg, W. Va., where he was a railroad employee. Born in Wood, W. Va., 1858-9-20. His father was Abraham Deem, born in Penn., his mother, Elizabeth (Guinn) Deem, born in Augusta Co., Va.

Children of Emily Ann Shotwell:

1. ADA MAY MOORE, born 1883-3-24, married to Claude Morris, 1908-3-21, and went to Zanesville, O., to live.

2. FRANK EZEKIEL MOORE, born 1885-12-7.

6 SARAH ASENATH SHOTWELL, born 1863-3-11. Educated in common school and in Tupper's Plains and Coolville Seminaries, Athens Co., O. Taught five years in said county and then went west, Oct. 14th, 1891. Began teaching in December, at Conastota, S. D. Taught there one year, two years in the district schools of McCook Co., one year in the country schools of Minnehaha Co., and two years in the public schools of Lenox, all in South Dakota.

Married 1897-6-16, at Sioux Falls, to GEORGE E. GROENVELD, born in East Friesland, Germany, and son of J. J. and Gertrude (Klugkist) Groenveld, both of East Friesland, Germany.

After marriage they lived 60 days on a "claim" in Charles Mix Co., then "proved up" and went to Lenox, S. D., where their home is 1909. After going west her time was occupied in teaching and in attending institutes in vacation. Went to the World's Fair in 1893.

In April, 1893, she bought a half interest in a quarter section of land in McCook Co., S. D., for $600. Sold it in 1901, for $1200. Then invested the money in a half interest with her husband in 240 acres in Roberts Co.

Says: "My husband had a little girl 6 years old which we loved and worked for but she was taken from us by the spinal meningitis, at 13 years."

In August, 1899, her brother, Edgar, took his motherless little girl, two and one-half years old and gave her to them. She "has always held to the Quaker teachings of her parents." Husband a Presbyterian.

"He is a breeder of full-blooded stock and manages his farms." She says they "have a very pleasant home." Husband a great reader, keeps well informed on questions of the day."

7 ISAAC SHOTWELL, born 1865-9-10. Common school education. Went west. Married VIVIAN SHERMAN at Seneca, Kan., 1890-10-30, daughter of Charles Auson and Sarah (Rockway) Sherman, both natives of Pennsylvania.

She was born in Erie Co., Penn., where she lived and at Nemeha, Kan., till marriage. Educated in common schools.

After marriage they lived in Kansas in '91 and '92, then in Oklahoma, then in Kansas till Isaac's death by drowning in Blue River, Kan., Aug. 17, 1903. In 1904 she went to Oklahoma where her home still was January, 1909. P. O. Terrelton, Pawnee Co., Oklahoma.

Children of Isaac Shotwell:

1. EMILY MAY, born 1891, at Seneca, Kan. She began teaching school before seventeen, in fall of 1908.
2. SARAH LAFRETTA, born ———— at Kansas City, Kan.
3. MARK OLON, born ———————— at Kansas City, Kan.

Vivian Shotwell is a member of the Christian Union church. Had been secretary and treasurer of Sunday School for four years in 1909.

8 EFFIE ELLEN, born 1867-12-8. Educated in common schools. Married 1888-9-2, to WALTER EDGINGTON DUNFEE, son of David and Elizabeth (Johnson) Dunfee and born 1860-5-20, near Torch, Athens Co., O. Soon after marriage in Sept. '88, they went to Creston, Ia., and came back in April, 1891. While west he was fireman on a railroad but has been a farmer since.

Has 100 acres of land one-half mile south of Torch, but for several years (July, 1909) has been living with her mother on the old Doan homestead in the same township and county and tending her farm.

Children of Effie (Shotwell) Dunfee:

1. HAZEL BELL, born 1890-1-20, at Creston, Ia.
2. ZOLA MARINE, born 1891-12-17, in Athens Co., O.
3. NELLIE RUTH, born 1894-5-2, in Athens Co., O.

4. LELA AGNES, born 1899-4-4, in Athens Co., O.

5. HERMAN SHOTWELL, born 1902-8-22, in Athens Co., O.

6. WILMA ETHEL, born 1905-12-10, in Athens Co., O.

9 EDGAR THOMAS SHOTWELL, born 1870-6-6. Educated in common schools. Married 1st, 1893-1-7, near Filmore, Decatur Tp., Washington Co., O., Lillian Bell Johnson, daughter of Alex Johnson, a native of that Tp., and Bell (Tibals) Johnson, a native of Carthage Tp., Athens Co., O. Lillian was born in Union Co., S. D., 1873-10-17. They first lived on his father's farm. Then in Marietta, O., from May, '95, to June, '99.

Children of First Wife:

1. OSCAR A. SHOTWELL, born 1894-8-5, and died 1895-6-5.
2. FAYE SHOTWELL, born 1896-12-22.

The mother died 1899-10-29, near Filmore. Edgar went to Lenox, S. D., about Aug. 1st, 1900, taking his little girl, Faye, with him which he gave to his sister, Sarah A. Groenveld and her husband. He lived at Lenox, till October, 1902. Then at Sioux Falls, S. D., till June, 1903, at Fessenden, S. D., till October, same year. Then at Garrison, N. Dakota, to date of report, Feb., 1909, except a little time on a claim.

Married 2nd, at Garrison, N. D., MABLE CLAIR HAYCROFT, 1907-10-8, daughter of Samuel Pierson Haycroft, born in Ill., and Carolina (Smally) Haycroft, born in New York. After their marriage they lived on a claim 8 miles west of Garrison, till Nov. 30th, 1908, and at Garrison since.

A carpenter, Republican. Wife member of Baptist church.

III JAMES DOAN, born 1832-2-22, in Bristol Tp., Morgan Co., O., and lived with the family as related in the life of his mother, Asenath Hampton Doan.

Educated in common schools and at a select school at Coolville, O. Married 1st Ann Elizabeth Wilson, daughter of Isaac and Elizabeth Wilson, of Decatur Tp., Washington Co., O., 1854-4-2, who died 1855-5-4. Lived on and tended his father's farm in Troy Tp., Athens Co., O. Went to Iowa in fall of '55, and returned about the winter of '56-7. Was wounded in one knee while in Iowa, by the kick of a horse. Not able to continue farm work, he traded land he had bought in Iowa, for a country store at Torch, Troy Tp., about two miles from his father's home.

Married 2nd, REBECCA GAD, 1857-6-14, daughter of George and Hannah (Van Fleet) Gad of Wesley Tp., Washington Co., O. The father, a native of Monroe Co., O., and the mother of Virginia, near Richmond.

James and Rebecca first lived at Torch, but moved about 1858, to Wesley Tp., Washington Co., where he resumed farming. Returned later and tended his father's farm. Bought land adjoining and lived on it a good many years but later on another farm he had bought in the neighborhood.

Rebecca (Gad) Doan was born 1830-9-30, in Washington Co., O., and died 1884-6-6. She was a good woman. A Methodist but later for convenience joined the United Brethren.

Children of James and Rebecca (Gad) Doan:

1 HAVILAH, born 1858-7-26. Common school education. Married to NATHAN FREEMAN BATCHELDER, 1880-6-16, born 1854-10-18, and son of Ebenezer and Ursula (Nuel) Batchelder, natives of Decatur, Washington Co., O.

Havilah and husband lived in several places in Athens Co., one in Washington and one in Hocking, moving many times. She joined the Methodist church at Torch but moving without certificate joined the Spiritualists with her husband, elsewhere.

Husband's occupation has been farming mostly, coal mining a while and railroading two and one-half years or more. Member of Odd Fellows and Foresters of America. Joined A. P. A's in 1883. Republican.

Children of Havilah (Doan) Batchelder:

1. SARAH EMILY, born 1881-3-4. Graduated in a school at Buchtel, Athens Co., and took a course in a commercial correspondence school at Scranton, Penn. Has been a clerk in stores and post offices. At the Plains Post Office, Athens Co., O., January, 1909.

2. LEWIS ELMER, born 1884-12-7, and died 1885-3-24.

3. FANNY ETHEL, born 1886-6-27. Has fair common school education. At home, January, 1909.

4. EDWARD FREEMAN, born 1889-10-17. "Has a good education for the time he spent in school. Worked at mining coal at Jobs, Hocking Co., and attended night school and can help his brother in his school work." Is working now on the railroad (1909).

5. JOHN EPHRIAM, born 1894-10-7. Still at school at home in Troy Tp., Athens Co., O. (Jan., 1909).

2 DEBORAH DOAN, born 1861-5-24, and died 1864-11-6.

3 GEORGE WILLIAM DOAN, born 1864-7-8, in Athens Co., O. Educated in common school only, but wanted a better education. Married Anna Flora Walden, 1895, daughter of William and Hester Maria (Purviance) Walden, and born 1867-1-26. Father born in Athens and mother in Jefferson Co., O.

Besides farming, George Doan, has been a dealer in real estate and taken many oil and coal "options." He has held township office and been notary public, joined a grange and has been lecturer. Has been church clerk and held Sunday School offices.

Republican. Congregationalist.

Wife a Baptist but in November, 1905, "came by letter into the Congregational church for convenience" and to be with her husband. They have lived since marriage near the old Doan homestead in Troy Tp., Athens Co., O.

Children of George W. Doan:

1. OLIVE GLADIS, born 1887-1-30. Educated in common school. Married to Floyd H. Morris, 1906-5-8.

2. STELLA MINONA, born 1889-6-21.

3. CLARA BERNICE, born 1891-6-2, died 1908-6-8. Had lived with grandparents in Coolville, for five years, over two being after the death of her grandmother which devolved much care of the grandfather upon her. A very good student. Studied hard and was prepared to teach but too young to receive a certificate.

A Baptist but a worker in a Methodist Sunday School. Was a young Christian worker much esteemed.

4. FLOSSIE RUTH, born 1897-5-8.

5. GEORGIE HESTER, born 1899-7-23.

6. PERRY ALTON, born 1904-4-8, died 1905-8-23.

7. E. DANA MILFORD, born 1906-7-18.

4 ISRAEL WALLACE DOAN, born 1869-9-10, in Troy Tp., Athens Co., O. Educated in common school and at Coolville High School. (Coolville is two and one-half miles from his father's and in Troy Tp., Athens co., O.) Received a diploma from Coolville Business Institute, March 21st, 1889. The following memorandum shows his struggle for an education. Aug. 1st, 1886, left home (not quite 17 years old) and worked twenty-four and one-half days. Then started to school at Torch. (Torch is about two miles from his father's.) Took measles in a few weeks and lay till spring. Apr. 4th, '87, went to work on a farm near Torch. June 5th, '87, went to Uncle Abiram Mains, in Morgan Co., to work on a farm. Oct. 31st, returned and attended school at home. April 9th, '88, entered Normal School at Coolville, for 10 weeks. Sept. 3rd, entered High School at Coolville. Did janitor work to meet expenses. Spring of '89, canvassed Athens Co., for Eureka Mowing Machine Co. July 29th, '89, entered Normal School, at Guysville, O. Sept. 30th, '89, went to

Buchtel, O., to work on Hocking Valley R. R., as a section hand. Nov. 22, '89, began to clerk in a produce house in Gallipolis, O. July 6th, '91, entered Normal School. Aug. 25th, '91, returned to railroad work at Nelsonville, O. January 8th, '92, began to clerk on a wharfboat at Gallipolis. Worked one week and then went to Coolville and he and his brother George rented their father's farm.

Married SARAH BELINDA KELLEY, 1892-2-25, at Court House in Athens Co., O., born 1866-11-3, at Pine Grove Farance, Scioto Co., O., and daughter of Isiah and Nancy Rebecca (Neal) Kelley. The father born 1839-8-10 in Taylor Co., Va., of Protestant Irish descent. The mother born 1848-1-10, at Sandford, Galia Co., O., of Scotch descent.

In July, 1892, bought part of his father's farm. April 2nd, 1895, started a milk diary at Ravenswood, W. Va., but returned to farm Oct. 1st, '97. Oct. 2nd, 1899, went to Jackson, O., to solicit for the Western and Southern Life Insurance Co., of Cincinnati, O. Worked for the company there and at Buchtel, Troy, Greenfield, Circleville and Martinsferry, all in Ohio. Resigned May 6th, 1907. May 20th, 1907, hired to Columbus Railway and Light Co., as conductor, where he still is (1909). Owns a 5-room house there and a 6-room house in Circleville, O. Says: "My sole object now is to give my children the education I would liked to have had.

In politics, Republican. In church fellowship, Disciple. Wife a Methodist.

Children of Israel W. Doan:

1. VERNA OTHELLA, born 1893-6-29, near Coolville, O. Member of United Evangelical church. Her pastor said to a neighbor that he wished all the girls in his church were like Verna Doan. Plays piano in absence of regular organist.
2. ORVILLE EVERETT, born 1895-4-25, at Ravenswood, W. Va. In same church with Verna. Carries newspapers after school.

3. LETTIE ELLEN, born 1896-11-5, died 1897-1-10.

4. HARRY ISAIAH, born 1897-5-27, near Coolville, O. Sometimes helps brother carry papers.

5. GEORGE THOMAS, born 1901-11-1, at Troy, O., and died 1902-11-11, at Circleville, O.

6. JOHN KELLEY, born 1905-3-5, at Circleville, O.

7. RALPH WALDO, born 1908-11-27, Columbus, O.

5 ABIRAM MAINS DOAN, born 1872-9-4, and died 1891-11-17.

James Doan married 3rd, 1884-11-9, Rebecca Tippy nee Moore and daughter of Ezekiel and Margaret (Elliott) Moore.

Children of James Doan and Third Wife:

1. ALFRED TYSON, born 1885-8-25.

After his father's death, Tyson helped his mother on the farm two years. From September, 1904, to March, 1905, was fireman on the B. & O. Southwestern R. R. Farmed at home again, April 1905, to October, 1906. Then conductor on a street car (at Columbus, O. (?)) till September, 1908. Then inspector in rubber works at Akron, O., till October, 1909. Then in cigar business in Columbus, O., till date of report, October 15, 1910. Married at Columbus, O., VESTA W. SNYDER, born at New Berlin, O., October 13, 1890, and daughter of Preston B. and Susan Adaline (Baker) Snyder. He was born at Union Town, O., April 17th, 1870, She at Canton, O., Feb. 28, 1865.

Child: Daisy May Doan, born May 16th, 1910, at Columbus, O.

2. ASENATH, born 1886-12-10, and died 1886-12-12.

3. OSCAR JOHN, born 1888-8-4. Was in a newspaper office as printer in the winter of 1909.

4. ANNA MAY, born 1890-2-4. Left without care of father or mother, lived at Dr. France's at Coolville. Attended school as she could. Was a good student highly

esteemed by her teacher. Got a certificate as teacher and a school in fall of 1908, for 8 months at $40 per month.

5. ALTA JEANETTE, born 1892-2-6.

6. ADA REBECCA, born 1893-11-6.

7. ARTHUR, born 1895-5-4.

8. ALBERTA ALICE, born 1900-5-10.

James Doan was a very industrious, economical, hard-working man who provided well for the physical wants of his family. Naturally endowed with the gift of government, he governed his children and his horses well and would get a great amount of work out of his team without apparent injury.

He took an interest in family history. Corresponded with some who were gathering material for the first edition of the "Doane Family" and furnished some if it.

He was in very feeble health for several years and suffered much. Died 1902-9-14. Republican. Though he once joined the United Brethren to be with his second wife in church fellowship, yet he seemed to adhere to the Friends. Observed their custom of silent worship at meals to the last.

IV ANN HAMPTON DOAN, born 1834-2-12, in Bristol Tp., Morgan Co., O. Married to William P. Doan, son of Milton and Ruth Anna (Slack) Doan, 1854-11-2, at Athens, O. Went to Iowa same month. Returned Dec. 11th, 1857. He went into partnership in March, 1858, with his uncles in farming and wool growing, on the old Doan homestead in Meigs Tp., Muskingum Co., O., and accumulated property. Was school director 12 years and township trustee 9. Was also church and parsonage trustee at Lytlesburg, Methodist Episcopal church, but did not become a member till 1901. Died of cancer, 1902-1-26.

Ann H. Doan married 2nd, James Howard, 1905-6-28, at her home in Lytlesburg, Muskingum Co., O. A farmer living near. A good man and very kind husband. Member of Methodist Protestant church.

Children of Ann:

1. BENAJAH DANIEL DOAN, born 1859-8-10, in Meigs Tp., Muskingum Co., O. Married 1880-9-20, Sarah Alta Simons, daughter of Charles Spellman and Margaret (Blackburn) Simons.

Benajah was reared on a farm but after marriage became successively, merchant, lumberman and telephone builder and manager and rents his farms.

2 SOPHIA DOAN, born 1862-8-25, married to Israel Milton Doan, son of Ulysses and Ann Pierpoint (Hampton) Doan at Hutchinson, Kan., 1880-8-25. Returned to Ohio but went again to Kansas. She returned a second time to Ohio and has lived at Lytlesburg.

Children:

1. WILLIAM CLARENCE DOAN, born 1889-8-15, in Meigs Tp., Muskingum Co., O. Attended Common School and engaged in farming and telephone work prior to 1908, when he entered Mt. Union College, Sept. 22nd. Had married Lizzie Mary Trott, of Pleasants City, Guernsey Co., O., 1907-8-27, at Newport, Ky. Still in college, winter of 1910.

2. HARRY MILTON DOAN, born 1894, at Sterling, Kan. In school (1909). Ann H. D. Howard has long been a member of the Methodist Episcopal church and a tender-hearted, dutiful daughter, sister, wife and mother. Helped much in gathering information for family history, both of the Doans and the Hamptons.

MARY ANN HAMPTON, (John 3, John 2, Joseph 1) married Elihu Robins as related on page 43.

Children:

I ZACHARIAH HAMPTON ROBINS, born 1839-12-11 in Morgan Co., O., married Lizzie Pine, 1870-6-8.

Children:

1 Lucy M., 2 Edith, 3 Florence, 4 Fred W., 5 Grace, 6 Arthur Elihu.

Lucy M. married to Geo. S. Twiggs, 1894-12-31. One child, Lester.

II WILLIAM DOAN ROBINS, born 1842-4-3, in Morgan Co., O. Unmarried. Was soldier in the civil war; "carries a rebel bullet," his mother says. "Was in public business a good deal at Cedar Rapids, both in county and city offices."

III CLARA ASENATH ROBINS, born in Morgan Co., O., 1843-11-23, and died 1880-4-23. Married to Robert Henry Whitnak, 1863-12-15.

Children:

1. Roger S., 2 William B., died at 10 months, 3 Luella, 4 Mary.

Roger married Cora A. Conley, 1891-1-14, one child, Clara L. Luella Whitnak married to Wm. H. McClure, 1891-6-30. Children: "Four in all." Two living, Hattie Luella and Henry William.

4. MARY WHITNAK married to Robert J. McCaw, 1891-5-7. Two children, Gladys and Donald.

IV ANNA E. ROBINS, born 1846-10-9, unmarried and at home, Feb. 1st, 1889, the date of her mother's letter. Also at the time of Edward Doan's visit. A Presbyterian. Died 1895-11-21.

V OLIVER W. ROBINS, born 1850-7-14, at Cedar Rapids, Ia. A carpenter. Married Sarah E. Whitnak, 1872-7-8.

Two children: Isabella C., and Bessie.

Bessie married to Edwin C. Monilow, 1896-9-17.

VI ASA H. ROBINS, born 1853-2-26, at Cedar Rapids, Ia. Married Jennie L. Whitnak, in 1883-3. One child, Flora L. He died about 1885. "His widow married again and did well," (her mother-in-law says) "he being good to her and the child." "They live in Massachusetts."

It has been cause of deep regret to the compiler of this history that he has been unable to get more information about the children and grandchildren of his aunt, Mary Ann Robins. He has written several letters in an effort to obtain more. Two of them sent to two of her sons, neither of whom replied.

Sixth Generation

61 NATHAN POYNER (6) HAMPTON, (James Hiram 5, James 4, John 3, John 2, Joseph 1), born 1853, at Gilbertville, Blackhawk Co., Ia. At the age of 8 years, went with parents to Burlington, Coffee Co., Kan. At 11 years to Lawrence, Kan., and got there next day after Quantrell's terrible raid and butchery. About a year later, to Cedar Rapids, Linn Co., Ia. At 14 to Raymond, Blackhawk Co., "while there received a common school education." "At 19, attended a high school at Waterloo, Ia." "A year later studied photography there. About 1874 the family moved to Akron, Plymouth Co., Ia., where he followed that business." Here, 1878-12-14, married Laura Christy, daughter of Robert and Mary Christy and born 1860-11-1.

In 1879 moved to Marion, S. D., and followed the barber's trade," which he continued at Elk Point, S. D., in '86. That fall he and brother Elmer built a flat boat there and put his family and goods on board, bound for Arkansas. Floated down the Missouri river about 8 weeks, "attended with considerable adventure and quite a few hairbreadth escapes." At St. Joseph, Mo., left boat and took to cars. In September "took up" land on White River, 8 miles east of Rogers, Ark. Lived on farm two years. Moved to Rogers and engaged in the barber's business.

In '91, began keeping hotel at Clinton, Henry Co., Mo. In '93 made an unsuccessful run for a home in the Cherokee country. Located at Ponea City, Kay Co., as barber, three years. Then as merchant on small scale but did well till all was lost by fire. In 1900 went to the "Kiowe, Comanche and Apache opening," and got a small piece of land in Washita Co., Oklahoma. When he had proved it went to Binger, Caddo Co., in 1904, and engaged in barbering. Became a member of the Knights of Pythias at Rogers and was serving as Chancelor Commander, when he left there. Is a member of the order of Modern Woodmen.

Children:

I IRA LEROY, born 1879-12-12, at Marion, S. D.
II MILLIE MAY, born 1881-9-2, at Akron, Ia.
III EVA LAURA, born 1885-12-8, at Akron, Ia.

62 AMY ALICE (6) HAMPTON, (James Hiram 5, James 4, John 3, John 2, Joseph 1), born 1857-10-8, at Waterloo, Ia. Lived in several places with parents. Educated in common schools till '74, when one year in Waterloo High School. Finished teaching her first term just before her eighteenth birthday. Taught and went to school alternately till fall of '78. "Went to Cedar Falls and attended Iowa State Normal School one term but was compelled to return home on account of great hardship caused by visitation of grasshoppers. Taught till '81. Then served as postmistress, at then Portlandville, now Akron, Ia., until married 1882-7-24, in Union Co., S. Dakota, but near Akron, Ia., to George Vincent Ellis, son of Ira and ——— (Judkins) Ellis, of London. After marriage lived at several places where her husband practiced medicine. At Caliope, in '82. At Hawarden '82 to '88, at Akron '88 to '96. At Canton, Miss., '96 and '97. Back to Akron in '97 and thence to Medical Lake, Washington, in 1903.

Episcopal Methodist and has served as Sunday School teacher, Junior Epworth League President, Superintendent of Junior Temple, etc.

Children of Amy Alice (Hampton) Ellis:

I HIRAM IRA ELLIS, born 1884-11-5, at Haverton, Ia. Was attending Washington State College in 1906.

II RINALDO VINTON, born 1888-12-5, at Akron, Ia.

Attending High School at home, Medical Lake, Washington, in 1906.

"Both boys stalwart fellows and exceptionally musical."

63 JAMES ELMER (6) HAMPTON, (James Hiram 5, James 4, John 3, John 2, Joseph 1), born 1864-1-7, in Coffee Co., Kan. Lived there and in several places in Iowa with his parents as related in life of his father. Attended Yanktown College, S. D., two years, 1885 and '86. Quitting school on account of the lack of means he taught school and clerked in a store till he had saved sufficient to go again. He entered the University of Michigan, Law Department, in the fall of 1890, and attended one year. The next years, finding an opportunity to assume the management of a college boarding house and thereby assist his sisters, Carrie and Nettie, to enter college, he undertook the task and with these two sisters, entered the University of the Northwest, now called Morning Side College, at Sioux City, Ia., the girls in the literary and himself in the law department, the girls also assisting in the boarding house, where all continued till he graduated.

He was admitted to the bar by the Supreme Court of Iowa, in May, 1892, and commenced practice at Akron, Ia., which he continued there ten years when he gave up practice because of a partial deafness which had grown on him to such an extent as to make it difficult to do that kind of business.

In July, 1902, he moved to Warwood, Minn., on the Lake of the Woods, and with a partner, engaged in general merchandise. Burned out in May, 1904, a total loss. He then engaged in the same business there on his own account on a smaller scale, which he continued till March, 1908, when he moved to Wanatchee, Washington.

Married 1894-10-4, at Akron, Ia., Mrs. Leila Hughes, nee Shirk, daughter of Frank S. and Celista (Hodges) Shirk and born 1869-11-12, at Greenfield, Ia., her parents native place.

Her former marriage was to Wm. J. Hughes, at Greenfield, Ia., 1889-9-25. He died 1892-3-25. She brought into the family the child of her former marriage, Myrtle Lillian Hughes, born 1891-8-25, who assumes the Hampton name.

Children:

I ELMER FOY, born 1895-8-9, died 1896-2-19.
II HARRY NATHAN, born 1898-7-19 (or 14th).

James Elmer is a member of the Methodist Episcopal church. Says he has never used intoxicating liquors in any form, nor tobacco in any form nor used profane language in his life and believes that neither his father nor his father's brothers nor his own brother, ever swore an oath in their lives. Does not make this statement as a boast but as a tribute to the Quaker people for their careful training of children. Republican.

64

CELIA ANNETTA (6) HAMPTON, (James Hiram 5, James 4, John 3, John 2, Joseph 1) born 1868-4-25, near Raymond, Blackhawk Co., Ia. "At the age of seven years she was converted and joined the Methodist Episcopal church. Had a common school education and for one year attended Morning Side College.

Almost seven years were occupied in teaching. Married 1893-6-29, to Rev. Justus Burdett Smith, at Akron, Ia. He is of New England stock and born 1858-5-21, at Nothingham, N. H. Is descended from Pierre Le Brun."

Their first home was at Akron, then at Holly Springs, Ia., '94-5. Mt. Hope, '95-6. Lecturing and preaching in the south, Sept., '96 to Sept., '97. Twin, Ia., Sept., '97 to June, '98. Traveling in Iowa, June, '98 to March, '99. Le Mars, Ia., two years.

Ill health made it needful to go to mountainous regions. Homestead land was found near Wenatchee, Washington, whither they went in April, 1902, and where their home was in 1906, with health restored. "She has been interested in church work all her life, holding herself ready for any duty called upon to do and counts herself happy in His name."

Has been Sunday School Superintendent, president of Missionary societies, Epworth League President and Junior Epworth League Superintendent. "But she feels the greatest responsibility placed upon her is to be the mother of four children to train for God."

Children of Celia Annetta H. Smith:

I RUTH LORENA SMITH, born 1894-4-23.
II REUEL JUSTICE SMITH, born 1895-7-5.
III HIRAM TRIMBLE SMITH, born 1899-6-16.
IV MARY ALVENA SMITH, born 1905-10-28.

65

CAROLINE ASENATH (6) HAMPTON, (James Hiram 5, James 4, John 3, John 2, Joseph 1) born 1872-12-3, in Blackhawk Co., Ia. "Her parents moved to Akron, Ia., in her early childhood where she grew to womanhood.

"She received what education she possesses in the public schools of Akron, in All Saints, an Episcopalian Boarding School, at Sioux Falls, S. D., and in Morning Side College, Sioux City, Ia., having attended the latter institutions one term each.

"She commenced teaching a country school at the age of seventeen and has taught in Iowa, Mississippi, N. Dakota, S. Dakota and Washington. She did not aspire to eminence as a teacher, however, because she never believed herself exactly suited to the work.

In 1902, she availed herself of the privilege of securing a homestead in N. Dakota, "commuting" in 1904. This she considers the only really interesting episode of her life. She has been mixed up with postoffice work, clerkship and proofreading.

She thoroughly enjoys living in touch with bread winners and endeavoring in a small way to help the "wheels go round." Unmarried (1909).

66 EMLEN (6) HAMPTON, (William 5, Zachariah 4, John 3, John 2, Joseph 1), born 1857-12-7, near Viola, Linn Co., Ia. Of his education he writes: "Quite limited as I only went to school about 21 months." Was a farmer in early life in Iowa. Went to Washington about the 10th of April, 1901, and lived at Poluce City. In 1903, went to Wenatchee, Washington. Occupation, farming and "orchard work." Church affiliation, Friends while in Iowa. Preached while with them. Since going to Washington, joined the "Christian" church. Holds no office but appoints meetings, prays and preaches, but without salary. "Never held civil office but was appointed guardian for his brother's property and once served as a juryman in Iowa. Unmarried (May 9th, 1908).

67 MARY ELIZA (6) HAMPTON, (William 5, Zachariah 4, John 3, John 2, Joseph 1), born 1863-9-26, near Viola, Linn Co., Ia.

She writes: "My education was limited to select schools at home till I was eighteen. I went for a short time to Maple Grove, (now Whittier) Winona, Ohio and Barnsville, O., Boarding School. Went to State College of Osteopathy, at Des Moines, Ia., 1-1-1901. Graduated there 1903-1-29. Post graduate course ended 6-29, same year. Practiced at Whittier, Anamosa and Coal Creek, and took care of her brother Zachariah and her father in their last sickness.

Went to Holton, Kan., 1908-4-4, to assist Alice Thompson make a home for the family of her cousin, Dana Ellis, whose children had lost their mother.

Of her church fellowship, she says: "I retain my right in the Smaller body of Friends who hold a general meeting in Philadelphia four times a year."

Unmarried (1909).

68 LEWIS (or Louis) PASEY (6) HAMPTON, (William 5, Zachariah 4, John 3, John 2, Joseph 1), born 1865-7-4, near Viola, Linn Co., Ia., died 1904-5-7, near Wenatchee, Washington.

In early life worked on a farm with his father. Married 1892-2-27, Anna Christine, daughter of Hans and Anna Margaret Pederson and born 1860-2-21, at Orten, near Varde, Denmark. Came to America with her parents in spring 1889. Father born 1830-7-29, mother 1835, both near Varde, Denmark.

Lewis and wife lived at Marion and at Greenwood farm, both in Linn Co., Ia., but moved to Wenatchee, Washington, 1901-10-24. Occupation, farming and fruit raising. He belonged to the Friends. Anna Christine, to the Lutherans. He was a Prohibitionist.

Children:

I HANS WILLIAM, born 1892-12-9, at Marion, Ia.

II ROY ALDEN, born 1895-6-8, at Greenwood Farm.

III JOHN LEWIS, born 1900-12-16, at Greenwood Farm.

All in Linn Co., Ia.

69

ADALINE ADELIA (6) HAMPTON, (Benjamin 5, Asa 4, John 3, John 2, Joseph 1), born 1857-10-5, near Waterloo, Blackhawk Co., Ia. Lost her father at five years of age and writes feelingly of his last visit home from the army on furlough and how he had to tear himself away from wife and children, never to return.

Married to THOMAS JEFFERSON KING, 1873-10-7, at Vinton, Ia., his birthplace. Father a native of Tennessee and mother of Indiana.

Occupation farming. Religion, Methodist. Politics, Democrat.

He died 1898-2-10, at Vinton, Ia.

Children of Adaline Adelia (Hampton) King:

I ELLA KING, born 1874-8-4, at Vinton. Married 1898-11-29, to Wm. Owens, a carpenter.

Children of Ella (King) Owens:

1. RUTH ADALINE, born 1899-5-29.
2. BLANCHE MINNIE, born 1901-11-1.
3. A daughter born 1908-8-4, on her mother's birthday.

II EARL LEROY KING, born 1877-6-13, at Vinton. Married Julia Anderson, 1898-2-12.

Child of Earl L. King:

1. LULU, born 1902-1-9.

III MABLE KING, born 1881-9-18. Married Wm. Anderson, 1897, "a foreman of section men." (Aug. 1908.)

Children of Mabel King Anderson:

1. ? BERT LORANE, born 1900-4-17.
2. ? OSCAR, born 1898-4-16.
3. ALICE, born 1907-1-19.

IV GEORGE HAMPTON KING, born 1885-3-13, at Vinton, Ia. Unmarried in August, 1908.

In Regular Army, Co. 63, Coast Artillery.

During her first husband's life they lived around Vinton. After a little over four years widowhood, she was married to Simeon Bailey, at Vinton, 1902-9-24, where they continued to live for two years. In 1904, they moved to Missouri and lived one year. In 1905, back to Vinton, Ia., on a farm. In 1907, back to Missouri, where they were in 1908. (P. O., Buffalo, Mo.)

Simeon Bailey is an old soldier. Was wounded at Columbia, S. C. Farmer, Baptist, Republican. Adaline is a Methodist.

70 ESTELLA VICTORIA (6) HAMPTON, (Benjamin 5, Asa 4, John 3, John 2, Joseph 1), born 1859-1-16.

She writes: "My mother married a second time when

I was between 14 and 15 years old and I had just a common education. When she married I learned dress making and worked at it till I married. At Tipton, Ia., where her mother then lived, 1881-6-15, married to LaFAYETTE LaMOTT, born 1852-6-28, at Clinton, Ia. His father, Alexander LaMott, was born in Paris, France. His mother, whose maiden name was Rosette Gruver, was born in Dayton, O.

After marriage they lived at Monmouth, Ia., 1882 to 1887. Then moved to Anamosa, and in 1889, to Unionville, Ia. From there in 1891, to Brighton, Ia., which was still their home in May, 1908. Both are members of the Methodist Episcopal church. Husband a farmer. Democrat.

Children of Estella Victoria:

I LULU LEE LA MOTTE, born 1883-9-18. Graduated in Brighton, Ia., High School, in 1903, and has been teaching ever since. (The mother wrote in May, 1908).

II MYRTLE ZELMA LA MOTTE, born 1885-2-6. Graduated in Brighton High School, in 1905. Has been teaching ever since except one term when she attended Iowa State Normal School at Cedar Falls.

III EARL HAMPTON LA MOTTE, born 1887-4-12. Quit school in the 10th grade.

IV GERALD CARLTON LA MOTTE, born 1889-2-2. Is still in school. (May, 1908).

V A little boy died at birth.

71 GERTRUDE (6) HAMPTON, (Benjamin 5, Asa 4, John 3, John 2, Joseph 1), born 1860-5-12, at Shellsburg, Ia. Education fair.

Married to ALBERT EDWARD HOLDEN, at Vinton, Benton Co., Ia., 1876-10-15, son of Breck M. and Mary Ann (Bixby) Holden. Father born at Ashtabula, O., and mother at Ruthland, Vt.

Children of Gertrude (Hampton) Holden:

I CHILTON ADRAIN HOLDEN, born 1878-12-30, died 1892-5-18.

II CLIFFORD HAMPTON HOLDEN, born 1880-8-19. A clerk and unmarried, May 1908.

III BLANCHE LE ALTA HOLDEN, born 1882-10-21. Married to Charles Bertran Cain, 1899-7-20, died 1901-5-20. Left a girl babe, born 1901-5-19, named Blanche Le Alta Cain. She was a musician of much ability. Especially a fine performer on the piano.

Her husband is a decorator.

IV FLORENCE FOY HOLDEN, born 1884-8-6, married to Elmer Thomas Good, 1904-7-27, a photo engraver in commercial work.

V CATO WADE HOLDEN, born 1880-4-20, married Sarah Violetta Lambert, 1908-1-11, born at N. Platte, 1890-1-26.

Gertrude and husband are Methodists. He is a Republican. Occupation, Denver City Tramway Co.

72 OLIVER ASA (6) HAMPTON, (Eli 5, Asa 4, John 3, John 2, Joseph 1), born 1854-11-9, in Iowa.

After traveling over the west for his health he finally located at Palasade, Col., where he spent the last nine years of his life in the mercantile business.

He died 1902-4-20, after a lingering illness of six years. (Rheumatism and complications). Buried at Marathon, Ia. Unmarried.

73 WILLIAM ALLEN (6) HAMPTON, (Eli 5, John 3, John 2, Joseph 1), born 1856-4-11, at Mt. Vernon, Ia.

At Iowa Falls, Hardin Co., Ia., 1879-11-26, married IDA BROWN, daughter of John Harrison and Mary Jane (Harmell) Brown, and born at Des Moines, Polk Co., Ia.

Father a native of West Virginnia, mother of Pennsylvania. They lived first at Spirit Lake, 1881 to '84, Marathon, till his death, 1890-6-12. Member of Baptist church. A farmer. Republican. Efforts to obtain fuller information unavailing.

Children:

I RUIA MAY, born 1880-8-13.
II MYRA, born 1884-2-2, died 1896-5-26, Marathon, Ia.
III ROY, born 1886-9-23, at Marathon, Ia.
IV GOLDIE, born 1887-12-12, died 1906-4-28 ,at Kansas City, Mo.

74

LINDLEY EDWARD (6) HAMPTON, (Eli 5, Asa 4, John 3, John 2, Joseph 1), born at Mt. Vernon, Ia., 1859-1-5.

Married RUIA SWARTWOUT, 1880-9-29, at Eagle City, Hardin Co., Ia., born at St. Lawrence, Jefferson Co., N. Y., 1861-8-29, and daughter of Samuel J. and Angeline (Merrill) Swartwout, both born in New York. Lindlay and wife lived at West Bend, Palo Alto Co., Ia., 1882 to '86. Marathon, Beunavista Co., Ia., '86 to December, 1894, when they moved to Palasade, Colorado, and engaged in fruit raising. In June, 1906, sold their possessions in Colorado and went to Los Angeles, Cal. Later went to Fullerton, Cal. A Republican.

Has held offices of Clerk and Deacon in the Bapist church. Wife also a Baptist.

Children:

1 VAY EDWARD, born 1883-11-20, at West Bend, Ia.
II ARNIE LORENZO, born 1885-8-13, West Bend, Ia.
III GEORGE LINDLEY, born 1888-4-17, near Marathan.

75

JESSE JAMES (6) HAMPTON, (Eli 5, Asa 4, John 3, John 2, Joseph 1), born 1865-10-5, at Mt. Vernon, Ia.

He writes: "After a happy home life until the age of twenty-three, I married MATTIE HIGHLY, 1888-10-

10, at Pickerel Lake, Beuna Vista Co., Ia., daughter of Thomas Jefferson and Jane (Welsh) Highly, and born at Logan, Hocking Co., O. Her father born at Chandlersville, Muskingum Co., Ohio.

"After seven years of successful farming in Iowa, moved to Palasade, Messa Co., Col., and engaged in raising fancy fruits, viz: cherries, apricots, peaches, grapes and apples."

Jesse and wife united with the Methodist Episcopal church, in 1892. He wrote in 1908: "Our four children are faithful members of the same church." He was Recording Steward then. A Republican.

Children:

I BLANCHE MAY, born 1889-7-6, near Marathon, Ia.
II LUCILE CORA, born 1891-6-8, near Marathon, Ia.
III ERWIN JESSIE, born 1894-10-27, near Marathon, Ia.
IV VERNA IDA, born 1899-7-9, at Palasade, Col.
V KERMIT MILLIKIN, born 1907-10-11, at Palasade, Col.

76

CHARLES HENRY (6) HAMPTON, (Eli 5, Asa 4, John 3, John 2, Joseph 1), born near Cedar Rapids, Ia., 1869-5-28.

Lived with parents at Cedar Rapids, Iowa Falls, Spirit Lake, Pickerel Lake, till twenty-one years old or later.

After his father's death rented the farm of his mother. Married at Marathon, Ia., 1893-6-4, HANNAH BLAYLOCK, daughter of Robt. Levol and Catharine Ann (Kester) Blaylock, and born 1874-10-8, at South English, Keokuk Co., Ia. Her father born in Ohio, and her mother in Pennsylvania.

He wrote in the summer of 1906: "My wife and I have been members of the Baptist church, for a little over 15 years. I am a deacon in the church. This is the second time, once was in Iowa. My wife and I have always been active workers in the church. Republican.

Children:

I EMORY WILLARD, born 1894-6-29.
II CLARA ELSIE, born 1896-2-26.
III BEULAH ELLEN, born 1898-1-11.
IV CHARLES ELDON, born 1900-9-7.

77 CLARA BELL (6) HAMPTON, (Eli 5, Asa 4, John 3, John 2, Joseph 1), born 1873-1-22, near Cedar Rapids, Ia. Eighth child and only daughter of Eli and Elmira Hampton. Says she had a fair opportunity for education. Married to WILLIAM LUTHER BARNS, 1901-6-10, at Pickerel Lake, Beuna Vista Co., Ia., son of John and Betsy Northop (De Wolf) Barns. Both parents born in Pennsylvania. Clara and husband lived at Plover, Pocohontas Co., Ia., then in Jan., 1902 moved to Palasade, Mesa Co., Col., and engaged in fruit raising in which they and her brothers were pioneers there. The husband had been a railroad conductor. Both are Baptists. He a Republican.

Children of Clara B. (Hampton) Barnes:

I EARLE HAMPTON BARNS, born 1894-4-12.
II LUTHER MADINE BARNS, born 1897-4-11.
III VIRGIL WILLIAM BARNS, born 1901-2-14.
IV HELEN PAULINE BARNS, born 1905-4-28.

78 ERNEST ELMER (6) HAMPTON, (Eli 5, Asa 4, John 3, John 2, Joseph 1), born 1876-9-13, near Iowa Falls, Hardin Co., Ia., and lived with parents there and at Spirit Lake and Pickerel Lake. "Was educated at the primitive country school house 1 1-2 miles away by a a school teacher of like quality."

"In his eighteenth year, "in June, 1894, he bade farewell to Iowa and all its fair charms and joined his brother, Oliver A., at Palasade, Mesa Co., Col. There they opened up a small stock of general merchandise. Continuing for three years. Sold out and engaged in fruit growing but finding out that he had missed his calling, bought back the old stand and went to selling merchandise again."

"The business growing until he and his partner found themselves working about 18 hours a day, assisted by five clerks and running two delivery wagons and his health failing, sold out in June, 1905. Since has been engaged in fruit growing and in selling real estate."

Married 1900-3-28, in Palasade, Col., MINA HATTES, daughter of Fred and Barbara (Dathan) Hattes and born at Mascouta, Ill., 1878-11-13. Father born at Gross Zimmern, Hesse-Darmstadt. Mother at Spice, Germany.

Child:

HELEN IMOGENE, born 1901-4-30.

79

EMMA LODISKEE (6) HAMPTON, (James 5, Asa 4, John 3, John 2, Joseph 1), born 1857-9-23, at Waterloo, Ia. Educated in common schools and at Iowa Wesleyan University. Married 1886-6-15, at Mt. Pleasant, Ia., to FRANK AYRES WEINER, of Stansbury, Mo., born 1855-12-23, near Marietta, O., and son of John and Cynthia Jane (Sprague) Weiner. Father born 1819, in Pennsylvania. Mother born in Ohio.

Emma and husband lived at Stansbury, from July 1st, 1886, to Aug. 1st, 1906. Were living in St. Louis, in 1909. Emma's husband was elected to the Missouri legislature twice. Served two terms and an extra session.

His occupation is newspaper work. Democrat. They are protestants but not members of church.

80

ELLA ALWILDA (6) HAMPTON, (James W. 5, Asa 4, John 3, John 2, Joseph 1), born 1860-2-29, at Liberty, Clark Co., Ia.

In her fourth year, was moved with parents, to Mt. Pleasant, Ia., where opportunities for education were good, finishing with the Iowa Wesleyan University.

Married to FRANK E. GREGG, at Mt. Pleasant, 1881-11-9, son of John M., and Emily (Bonar) Gregg, and Born at Burlington, Ia., 1858-1-2. His mother born at

Wheeling, W. Va. After marriage, Ella and husband, lived at Burlington, Ia., '81 to '84, Lincoln, Neb., '84 to '89, Salt Lake City, '89 to '92, Denver, Col., '92 to date of report, 1908. He is an attorney and a Republican. Both Presbyterians.

"In 1889, they spent several months traveling in Europe. In 1903, they made a trip through the Mediterranean, visiting various places including Spain, Greece, Turkey, Egypt, Palistine and Northern Europe."

Child:

I IMOGENE HAMPTON GREGG, born 1895-6-26.

81 HATTIE ANNETTA (6) HAMPTON, (James W. 5, Asa 4, John 3, John 2, Joseph 1), born 1863-12-15. Educated at Mt. Pleasant High School and at Iowa Wesleyan University. Married at Mt. Pleasant, Ia., 1885-6-9, to WINFIELD SCOTT BICKSLER, of Salem, Ia., son of John and Sarah A. (Buffington) Bicksler. Father born in Fairfax Co., Va., mother in Washington Co., Penn.

Hattie and husband lived at Boone, Ia., from June, 1885, to Oct. 1901, and Denver, Colo., from then to date, 1908. They attend "Divine Service Church." He is a Republican. Was graduated at Whittier College and Iowa City Law School. Occupation, attorney at law.

82 DANIEL WILLIAMS (6) HAMPTON, (Oliver 5, John 4, John 3, John 2, Joseph 1), born 1858-1-21, near Springville, Ia. Had common school education. Has followed farming all his life except about two years spent in California.

Married 1879-9-8, MARY S. VAIL, daughter of Jesse and Mary Jane (Southers) Vail, of Springville, Ia., and born 1860-6-9, in Belmont Co., O. Parents both natives of that place. Daniel has been president and secretary of a farmer's alliance and his wife secretary of some neighborhood clubs. He is an adherent of the Friends society and a Republican.

Children:

I ALFRED G., born 1881-3-4.
II LURA, born 1883-6-29.
III EARL D., born 1885-1-25.
IV MILLIE, born 1887-2-22, at Whittier, Cal. ,and died there 1889-8-29.
V FLOYD, born 1892-3-30.
VI HATTIE, born 1894-7-31.
VII DEAN, born 1897-5-21.

83 DELWIN C. (6) HAMPTON, (Oliver 5, John 4, John 3, John 2, Joseph 1), born near Springville, Ia., 1872-4-18. Educated in Friends school near home and attended Scattergood Seminary, West Branch, Ia.

A farmer. A Friend and a Republican.

Married 1896-11-18, EDITH C. COPPECK, daughter of Benjamin Coppeck, of Coal Creek, Ia., and born 1872-7-22. Her mother's maiden name was Esther Winder, of Carroll Co., O. Father also a native of Ohio.

Children:

I EVA LYDDA, born 1898-5-7.
II OLIVER B., born 1900-3-7.
III BERTHA, born 1903-5-5, died same year.
IV HOWARD J., born 1907-11-30.

84 WILBUR E. (6) HAMPTON, (Oliver 5, John 4, John 3, John 2, Joseph 1), born 1886-8-20, near Viola, Ia. A member of Friends Society and educated in their schools. Married 1907-8-21, ROSANNA MOORE, of Galena, Kan., daughter of Lee and Melissa (Ferguson) Moore. Father born in Warren Co., and mother in Clinton Co., O.

85 CHARLES CLYDE (6) HAMPTON, (Robert 5, John 4, John 3, John 2, Joseph 1), born 1886-6-21, near Springville, Ia. Educated in Friends' primary schools near home in Iowa and at Friends' Boarding School at Barnesville, O.

Married 1891-7-10, CORA ANNA ELYSON, daughter of Benjamin and Elma (Armstrong) Elyson, and born 1868-8-18, near West Branch, Cedar Co., O. Charles and Cora bought and settled on a highly improved farm near West Branch. "He follows farming but has taught quite a number of schools."

Both members of the Friends Society. Republican.

Child:

CLARA ELMA, born 1900-3-23.

86 EDGAR CLIFTON (6) HAMPTON, (Robert 5, John 4, John 3, John 2, Joseph 1), born 1867-12-19, near Springville, Ia.

Educated in Friends primary schools, at home and at their boarding school at Barnsville, O.

Married, 1890-2-27, AGNES BUNDY, daughter of Wm. Engle and Rebecca (Doudna) Bundy, born 1871-10-7. Father a native of Belmont Co., O. Edgar is an electrician. Lives at Marion, Linn Co., Ia., and is a member of the Board of the Cedar Rapids Telephone Co.

"He and his wife are members of the Methodist Episcopal church. Are temperance workers and Sabbath school teachers and officers." No children reported.

87 CHESTER LARUE (6) HAMPTON, (Robert W. 5, John 4, John 3, John 2, Joseph 1), born 1869-10-20. Educated in Friends' private schools near home in Iowa, and at Barnsville Boarding School, O. Married IRENE TEST 1895-9-12, daughter of Albert and Lydia Ann (Faucet) Test, and born 1872-3-21, near Salem, O. Parents both natives of Columbiana Co., O.

Chester and Irene were living in May, 1906, at Mitchel, S. D., and were "running a wholesale ice cream and sherbert and fancy candy factory." "Both members of the Methodist Episcopal church and active members of the Prohibition party." No children.

88 MARY DELITHA (6) HAMPTON, (Robert 5, John 4, John 3, John 2, Joseph 1), born 1874-2-22.

Educated in Friends' primary schools, at home, at West Branch Boarding School, Ia., at Westown Boarding School, Penn., and graduated at State Normal School, Cedar Falls, Ia.

Married 1902-12-25, to EDW. F. GAMBLE, of Winona, O., son of Samuel and Mary Jane (Fogg) Gamble, and born 1894-10-12, near Salem, O. Father born in Columbiana Co., O. Mother in N. Jersey. Mary D. and husband were living (in 1908) near Vivian, Lyman Co., S. D. Farmers, Friends, Prohibitionists.

Children: ERMA GENEVA and VIOLA, twins, and MARVIN A. All died in infancy.

"She died 1909-2-10, at Sioux City, Ia. Sick 8 years. Consumption.

89 WALTER JOHN (6) HAMPTON, (Robert W., 5, John 4, John 3, John 2, Joseph 1), born 1883-8-31. Educated in Friends' primary schools at home, at their Boarding School, at West Branch, Ia., and graduated at the Business College, Cedar Rapids, Ia. Is a stenographer and a school teacher. Friend, Prohibitionist. Unmarried, 1906.

90 CHARLES NEVIL (6) HAMPTON, (Edward 5, John 4, John 3, John 2, Joseph 1), born 1877-4-19, at Viola, Ia.

Attended college at Healdsburg, Col., for a while. Married, 1895-11-26, at Vinton, Ia., AMY LEMORA STRITE, daughter of Silas Page and Clara Elizabeth (Dunn) Strite, and born 1877-5-25, at Springville, Ia. Her father born at Mercer, Penn., and mother at Coldwater, Mich. Charles and wife lived at Topeka, Kan., but went to Lincoln, Neb., in 1906. In electric railroad service. Republican. Neither a member of church in 1908.

Child:

VERDA CLARE, born 1899-5-10.

"He traveled through the western states with his

parents and brother, visiting the Yellowstone Park in 1893. He wrote an account of this trip which was published in the Youths Instructor, about 1896, extending through nine numbers which was considered fine for one of his age."

91

FRANK JULIUS (6) HAMPTON, (Edward 5, John 4, John 3, John 2, Joseph 1), born 1883-2-24, at Osage City, Kan. Education limited by poor health in youth. Later he took up music. Married IDA VIVIAN CARLSON, 1905-11-5, at Lincoln, Neb., daughter of Carl Fred and Marie Catherine (Nelson) (?) Carlson, and born 1885-5-18, at Stockholm, Sweden. Parents both Swedes.

Frank is a musician. Orchestra and Band work. Won honor at band contest at Milwaukee, in 1905. He was permanently injured by overlifting when about 12 years old, which has caused much suffering through life. Have lived in Lincoln, Neb., since marriage. Neither member of church. He takes no part in politics. No children in 1908.

92

JEPTHA (6) HAMPTON, (Jonathan 5, Samuel 4, John 3, John 2, Joseph 1), born 1855-8-20, in Linn Co., Ia. Lived with parents in Linn and Keokuk counties. Educated in common schools.

Married ALICE WILLIAMSON, 1895-8-20, born at West Branch, Cedar Co., Ia., 1875-8-8, daughter of Joseph John and Alice Cary (Grawell) Heacock. Her mother died when Alice was about six weeks old and when about four (4) years old she was adopted by John Williamson and wife, hence her change of name. Her own father was born in Stark and mother in Logan Co., Ohio.

Jeptha and wife are Friends. He is a farmer. Republican. Wife has held office of treasurer of cemetery association.

Children:

I CECIL RICHARD, born 1896-6-12.

II MARION ARTHUR, born 1898-6-30.
III SARAH EVALINDA, born 1900-9-18.

93 LUCINDA MARSHAL (6) HAMPTON, (Jonathan 5, Samuel 4, John 3, John 2, Joseph 1), born 1857-7-3, in Linn Co., Ia., near Springville and lived with parents in Linn, Cedar and Keokuk counties. Educated in common schools. Married near Coal Creek, Ia., 1873-11-13, to FRANCIS HOWARD JONES, son of Obediah and Martha (Crumly) Jones, born 1853-10-30, near Richland, Ia. Father born in Blount and mother in Green Co., Tenn. Francis is a teacher and a farmer. Had taught 26 terms of school at date of report, winter of 1908. They had lived in Keokuk Co. '78 to '80, Warren Co. '80 to '82, Keokuk again '82 to '92, and from then to date, 1908, in Putman Co., Mo., six miles south of the Iowa line, where they have a farm.

Lucinda has been Overseer in Friends church and husband, elder, clerk and trustee. Had been superintendent of Sabbath School most of the time for 30 years.

Children of Lucinda M. (Hampton) Jones:

I ORPHA ALMEDA JONES, 1879-11-20, near Richland, Ia. Educated in common schools and Pleasant Plains Academy. Married to Geo. B. Daugherty, 1898-12-25.

Children of Orpha A. Jones:

1. WM. HOWARD DAUGHERTY, born 1900-2-1, near Omaha, Mo.

2. LEAH BLANCHE DAUGHERTY, born 1907-1-29, near Euphrata, Washington.

II ELIZABETH LEONA JONES, born 1884-6-24, near Richland, Ia. Educated in common schools and in Pleasant Plains Academy. Married to WM. BEALS, near Omeha, Mo., 1906-1-17. He graduated at Earlham Academy, Ia., Farmers.

Child of Elizabeth Leona:

1. WILLIAM THOMAS BEALS, born 1908-6-22.

III OLIE EMMA JONES, born 1887-8-1, near Hedrick, Keokuk Co., Ia. Educated in common schools and a few term at Chaper Academy.

IV LOREN ELWOOD JONES, born 1905-10-16, near Omeha, Mo.

94 ADDA ACHSA (6) HAMPTON, (Jonathan 5, Samuel 4, John 3, John 2, Joseph 1), born 1859-6-12, at Springville, Iowa.

Educated in common schools. Married 1880-8-11, to ELISHA CLAYTON JONES ,born 1851-5-8, in Blount Co., Tenn., brother to Frances H. Jones, husband of Adda's sister, Lucinda. They lived at Richland, from '80 to '90, at Coal Creek, '90 to 1900, then at Richland again to date, 8-8-1908. Farmers. Friends. Elisha has been elder for several years.

Children of Adda Achsa:

I VIOLA MABLE JONES, born 1881-8-24, at Richland, Ia. Educated in common schools. Married to FLOYD HIXON, 1904-2-8, at Fairfield, Jefferson Co., Ia. Hardware merchant.

Children:

1. VELDA MARIE HIXON, born 1905-5-19 at Fairfield.

II JESSE CLIFTON JONES, born 1883-1-21, at Richland. Had one year at high school. Farmer. Married Loverta Bond, 1905-1-11.

Children:

1. JAMES HARMON JONES, born 1906-3-30.

III JEPTHA HOWARD JONES, born 1887-11-30, at

Richland, Ia. Educated in common schools. Occupation, railroading. Married GRACE JOHN, 1906-9-26, at Colorado Springs.

Children:

1. DARYL CLAYTON JONES, born 1907-12-24.

IV ARLEIGH WILLARD JONES, born 1894-9-6, at Coal Creek, Ia. Had a common school education.

95 THOMAS ELWOOD (6) HAMPTON, (Jonathan 5, Samuel 4, John 3, John 2, Joseph 1), born 1861-12-20, in Cedar Co., Ia. Educated in district schools. Married 1892-8-12 to SARAH ESTHER MILLHOUSE, at Marshaltown, Ia., daughter of Isaac C. and Rachel (Yocum) Millhouse. Father born at Pennsville, O.

Elwood and wife lived about 9 years at VanCleve, Ia., at Marshalltown 5, and returned to Van Cleve, spring of 1907. Farmer and dealer in live stock.

Wife born at Pennsville, O., and educated in district school and Friends' Boarding School. Friends. Republican.

Children:

I WILLIAM ISAAC, born 1895-7-8.

II MYRTLE JONES, born 1897-2-6.

III EUNIA MELVA, born 1898-12-27.

IV THOMAS EDWIN, born 1900-11-2.

96 ELIZABETH (6) HAMPTON, (Jonathan 5, Samuel 4, John 3, John 2, Joseph 1), born 1866-4-20, in Linn Co., Ia. Calls her opportunity for education, limited. Married to BENJAMIN BRIGGS, 1899-7-15, at Coal Creek, Ia., son of Jonathan and Elizabeth (Millhouse) Briggs and born 1844-2-25, in Belmont Co., O. Jonathan Briggs was born in Jefferson Co., O. Her husband was raised a farmer but is mostly employed in some light mechanical work when able. Has been an invalid most of the latter part

of his life. They have not changed residence from Coal Creek, since marriage. Both Friends. Republican.

Child of Elizabeth (Hampton) Briggs:

1. WILLIAM BRIGGS, born 1900-2-15.

97 SARAH CARBEE (6) HAMPTON, (Jonathan 5, Samuel 4, John 3, John 2, Joseph 1), born 1870-7-7. Educated in country schools. Married 1905-4-10, to OWEN E. MILLER, at Whatcheer, son of Jas. and Harriet Eleanor (Moon) Miller. Both parents born in Ohio. Father in Perry Co.

Sarah and husband have lived since marriage in Keokuk Co., Ia. Neither is a member of church. He is a farmer and a Democrat.

Child:

1. OMA HARRIETT, born 1906-2-3.

98 JOHN WILLIAMSON. (6) HAMPTON, (Jonathan 5, Samuel 4, John 3, John 2, Joseph 1), born 1874-9-6, at Coal Creek, Ia.

"Attended common schools till 18 years old then went to Scatter Good Seminary two years. Married 1897-11-16, at Coal Creek, Ia., ELMA EDMUNSON, born in 1872, and daughter of John and Ruth (Heald) Edmundson. Both of Columbiana Co., O. John W's occupation is farming. Both are Friends.

99 NETTIE (6) HAMPTON, (Isaac Steer 5, Samuel Betts 4, John 3, John 2, Joseph 1), born 1868-6-20, at Viola, Ia. Educated in a grammar school. Married to DANIEL CLARKE Thanksgiving Day, 1888-11-28, at Wilmar, San Diego Co., Cal, son of Horace and Susan Thankful (Cole) Clarke, both of whom were born near Salt Lake City.

Children:

1. IDA MYRTLE CLARKE, born 1890-1-22, at San Borodino, Cal. She was attending high school in Nov. 1908, intending to fit herself for teaching.

2. WORMAN HAMPTON CLARKE, born 1895-3-28. This child died at the same place, 1903-5-24, from an injury caused by a fall from a bicycle the day before, riding home from Sunday School.

100 SAMUEL BETTS (6) HAMPTON, (Isaac Steer 5, Samuel Betts 4, John 3, John 2, Joseph 1), born 1870-2-26, near Viola, Ia. Educated in public schools. Married NORA WILLETTS, Thanksgiving Day, 1890-11-27. Educated in public schools and in Penn College, Osaboosa, Ia., and daughter of Gabriel B. and Jemima Elmira (Sheridan) Willetts, born 1868-3-6, at Amboy, Ind. Father born in Grant Co., and mother in Henry Co., Ind. Samuel and wife have lived at Wildmar, Riverside, Long Branch, Hollywood, Whittier and Carona, California. He has been in the citrous fruit business. Both are Friends.

Manager of Whittier Citrous Association, Oct., 1902 to Oct., 1905., of Corona Lemon Co., 1905 to date, 11-26-1908.

Children:

I ROBERT LESTER, born 1893-5-7, at Riverside, Cal.

II ETHYLIN ELLEN, born 1896-12-16, near Long Branch, Los Angeles Co., Cal.

III DORIS HELLEN, born 1898-9-30, at Riverside, Cal.

101 IDA (6) HAMPTON, (Isaac Steer 5, Samuel Betts 4, John 3, John 2, Joseph 1), born near Viola, Ia., 1872-11-12. Educated in common schools and graduated at high school, Pasadena, Cal. Married to Clarence Clyde Hiatt, on Thanksgiving Day, Nov. 24th, 1892, at Riverside, Cal., son of Robert Cooper and Sarah (Sharpless) Hiatt. Lived since marriage at Pasadena, Whittier, Berkley and

Corona, Cal. (Nov., 1908.) They were associated with the Friends at Whittier, but there being no Friends at Corona, they attend the Methodist church. She was President of the Willing Workers Society, at Whittier, and a Sunday School teacher. He was a foreman in a lemon packing house at date. (1908.)

Children of Ida:

I ROBERT CARROLL HIATT, born 1896-6-1, at Whittier, Cal.
II CHESTER HAMPTON HIATT, born 1901-3-25, at Berkley, Cal.

102 CORA BELL (6) HAMPTON, (Isaac Steer 5, Samuel Betts 4, John 3, John 2 Joseph 1) born 1876-6-25, at Sterling, Kan. Graduated from Preparatory Department of Whittier College, Cal.

Married to HORATIO THOMAS BANDY on Thanksgiving Day, Nov. 28th, 1900, at Des Palos, Mercede Co., Cal., son of Horatio Osborn and Melinda Rhoda (Ray) Bandy. Father from Illinois, mother from Missouri.

She was a Friend, now a Methodist, husband also a Methodist and a steward in the church. (Dec., 1908.) A Prohibitionist. A mechanic in a planing mill at Riverside.

Children of Cora Bell:

I FRANCES ELIZABETH BANDY, born 1901-12-17.
II MILDRED CATHARINE BANDY, born 1907-1-16.

103 WILLIAM EVERETT (6) HAMPTON, (Isaac Steer 5, Samuel Betts 4, John 3, John 2, Joseph 1), born 1892-6-6. A child of Isaac's second marriage. Had a twin sister Mary Edith, who died at three years. He is in his 18th year at this writing. (Jan., 1910.)

104 CLINTON ELMER (6) HAMPTON, (Richard B. 5, Samuel 4, John 3, John 2, Joseph 1), born 1864-10-21, near

Springville, Ia. Educated in common schools. Married SARAH E. SMITH, 1886-3-17, at Coal Creek, Ia., daughter of Evan and Mary (Burgess) Smith and born 1859-9-30, near Bartlett, O. Father born 1819-5-31, near Flushing, O. Mother near Smithville, O.

Clinton and wife lived at Gary, Kan., till spring of 1889, at Coal Creek, Ia., till spring of 1894, then near Dwight, 1889, at Coal Creek, Ia., till of 1894, then near Dwight, Kan., till report. (Nov., 1908.) Farmer. Was R. F. D. mail carrier 4 years and 8 months. Both are Friends. He has been Clerk of Preparative, Monthly and Quarterly meetings and she of Monthly and Quarterly meetings of Friends.

He has been president, treasurer and representative of a mutual telephone company at different times. Socialist.

Children:

I LOVISA M., born 1887-9-3, at Dwight, Kan.
II ELLEN, born 1889-3-30, at Dwight, Kan.
III ALVA JESSE, born 1891-10-11, at Coal Creek, Ia.
IV RUSSEL B., born 1896-8-25, at Dwight, Kan.

105

MARY JANE (6) HAMPTON (Richard B. 5, Samuel Betts 4, John 3, John 2, Joseph 1), born 1866-10-12.

Educated in common schools. Married DAVID HIATT, 1897-11-3, at Emporia, Kan., son of Elkana and Jane (Lee) Hiatt. Father born in Grant Co., Ind. Mother in Blount Co., Tenn. Mary Jane and husband lived at Toledo, Kan., after marriage. Moved to Washington. He was a merchant and farmer. Held office of postmaster at Toledo. Republican. Both Friends.

Children:

I LEE ROY HIATT, born 1898-9-9, at Toledo, Kan.
II RICHARD ORAM HIATT, born 1900-7-8.
III DAVID CLIFTON HIATT, born 1902-9-29.
IV LORA MARIA HIATT, born 1907-11-6.

106 JOSEPH (6) HAMPTON, (Richard B. 5, Samuel Betts 4, John 3, John 2, Joseph 1), born 1875-9-31, near Springville, Ia. Educated in common schools. Married ALMA DAY, 1898-12-28, at Emporia, Kan., daughter of Jesse Price and Telinda Jane (Pettyjohn) Day, and born 1878-11-1, at Moss Springs, Kan. Father born in Wells Co., and mother in Huntington Co., Ind.

Joseph and Alma lived near Dwight, Kan., three years. Moved to Oklahoma, March 1st, 1902. Moved back in fall of same year and to Alta Vista, Kan., spring of 1907.

Dealer in produce and feed. Formerly a farmer. Republican. Both members of "Church of Christ," often called "Campbellites."

Children:

I LILA E., born 1899-11-5, died 1899-11-10.
II NELMA FENTON, born 1905-1-4, at Alta Vista, Kan.

107 WILLIAM (6) HAMPTON (Richard B. 5, Samuel Betts 4, John 3, John 2, Joseph 1), born 1877-10-13, in Rice Co., Kan. Educated in public schools of Gary Co., Kan. Married NANCY ELIZABETH SHANNON, at Council Grove, Kan., 1901-6-23, daughter of Thomas Markin and Tabitha Jane (Saunders) Shannon and born near Sylvan Grove, Kan., 1878-6-23. Father born near Muncie and mother near Hartford, Ind. William and wife lived at Lind, near Dwight, Kan., till Nov., 1902. Then moved to Wenatchee, Washington. Members of the Seventh Day Adventist church. Non-partisan. Farmer. He has held office of clerk in his church several years.

Child:

I KARL ANDREW.

108 JOHN PIERPOINT (6) HAMPTON, (Richard B. 5, Samuel Betts 4, John 3, John 2, Joseph 1), born at Ster-

ling, Kan., 1880-1-16. Educated in "District School No. 22, Gary Co., Kan."

Married ORA ETHEL FURNEY, at Junction City, Kan., 1900-8-9, daughter of William Nathan and Catharine (Allen) Furney, and was born in 1882, in Morris Co., Kan. Both parents born in Putnam Co., Ind.

John and wife lived in Kansas. Moved from Kansas to Boulder, Col., spring of 1906, and the next fall to Wenatchee, Washington, "The Home of the Big Red Apples."

Occupation, ranching. Religion, Church of Christ. Democrat.

Children:

I ZELLA FOY, born 1903-3-6, at Alta Vista, Wabansee Co., Kan.

II HAROLD RICHARD, born 1905-8-31, same place.

III CLARA BELL, born 1908-6-18, at Wenatchee, Washington.

109

ANNA (6) HAMPTON, (Richard B. 5, Samuel Betts 4, John 3, John 2, Joseph 1), born 1882-3-26. Married to JAMES R. BARCROFT, at Wenatchee, Wash., 1903-5-6, son of William and Anna C. (Siebert) Barcroft, and born at Pittsburg, Pa., 1875-6-6. Father also born at Pittsburg.

Anna and husband have lived at Wenatchee, Washington, since marriage, to date. (January, 1910.) Both are Presbyterians. He is a fruit grower. Republican.

110

RUTH (6) HAMPTON, (Richard B 5, Samuel Betts 4, John 3, John 2, Joseph 1), born 1884-4-21, at Dwight, Morris Co., Kan. Educated in "country schools." Married to William Quinn, 1900-6-11, son of Bernard M. and Elizabeth A. (Burns) Quinn ,and born 1877-9-28, at Dwight, Kan. Father born at Eosopus, N. Y., mother at East Troy, Wis.

Ruth and husband lived at Alta Vista, Kan., about 18 months, at Wenatchee, Washington, 6 months, at Dwight,

Kan., 7 years at date. (Dec., 1908.) Farmers.

Children:

I EARL, born 1902-6-6, at Wenatchee, Wash.

II CLARENCE born 1905-9-7, at Dwight, Kan.

111 FRANK A. (6) HAMPTON, (William Steer 5, Samuel 4, John 3, John 2, Joseph 1), born 1873-12-19.

Letters to his father failed to bring any account of him or his whereabouts. Mary E. Bedell reported several years ago that he had been a commercial traveler and had lived at Davenport, Ia.

112 MAUD (6) HAMPTON, (William Steer 5, Samuel Betts 4, John 3, John 2, Joseph 1), born 1878-9-3. The same is true of her case as of Frank's in regard to her father's failure to answer inquiries. Ruth Quinn reported her to be a "graduated nurse."

113 MARY EMILY (6) HAMPTON, (Solomon E. 5, Cary 4, John 3, John 2, Joseph 1), born near Milton, Ky., 1873-5-2. She "completed the graded school course of Carroll Co., Ky., and the high school course of Louisville, Ky. She spent a year in Minneapolis, Minn., keeping house for her brother, Walton, and was at Salt Lake City, Utah, for the same purpose, in 1910. She is a Christian woman. A member of the Methodist Episcopal church South, and has held offices in its Sunday Schools, Epworth League and both its Home and Foreign Missionary Societies.

Was helpful to the writer of this history in gathering materials for it in a very cheerful and obliging manner.

114 MOSES JACKSON (6) HAMPTON, (Solomon Ernest 5, Cary 4, John 3, John 2, Joseph 1), born 1875-2-28, near Milton, Ky. Received the degree of B. S. at Hanover College, Indiana, in 1896.

After going into business for himself, was traveling Salesman in Minnesota two and a half years, 1894-7.

Since then has been farming and stock-raising with his father. (Dec., 1909.)

Master of Milton Lodge No. 461 F. & A. M., A. D. 1904. Secretary of same since December, 1907. Elected Grand Representative of the same lodge to Grand Lodge of Kentucky, 1908 and 1909.

115 ELLA KATE (6) HAMPTON, (Solomon E. 5, Cary 4, John 3, John 2, Joseph 1).

Educated in Carrol Co., Ky., schools and in high school of Madison, Ind. She took a lively interest in the preparation of the Hampton History. Sent the writer items of value and cheerful, encouraging letters.

"A Christian woman. Member of the Methodist Episcopal Church South. Interested in and connected with all branches of church work."

116 BESSIE PAYNE (6) HAMPTON, (Solomon E. 5, Cary 4, John 3, John 2, Joseph 1), born 1878-12-6, near Milton, Ky.

Educated in public schools of Carroll Co., Ky., and in high schools of Carrollton, Ky., and Madison, Ind.

Married MICHAEL EGGLESTON GARBER, of Madison, Ind., 1904-12-22, son of Michael Christian and Blanch Eggleston (Goode) Garber.

Bessie is a member of the Baptist church and has held minor offices therein, at Milton, and in the Ladies Society of the Presbyterian Church, at Madison, Ind.

Husband a Republican. Manager of the Madison, Ind., Courier, at date. (Jan. 1910).

Children:

I BESSIE HAMPTON GARBER, born 1906-6-9.

II CAROLINE EGGLESTON GARBER, born 1909-12-16, and died 1909-12-25.

117 HARVEY MOORE (6) HAMPTON, (Solomon E. 5, Cary 4, John 3, John 2, Joseph 1), born 1880-8-6, in Carroll Co., Ky.

Educated in country schools of Carroll Co., and in high school of Madison, Ind. Coming of age, he worked for his father on a farm 1901 to 1907. Married 1907-3-6, at the Methodist Church South, Milton, Ky., NANNIE WILLIS, daughter of John Pugh and Nannie (Pryor) Willis, and born 1879-5-26, in Trimble Co., Ky. Father born at Madison, Ind., mother in Trimble Co., Ky.

Since marriage he is in partnership with J. P. Strother, dealing in coal, fertilizers, farm implements and hardware.

Harvey and wife are members of the Methodist Episcopal Church South. He has filled the Chair in the Masonic Lodge, No. 461, Milton, Ky. Wife has taught school.

Children:

I ERNEST MOORE, born 1908-3-3.
II VIRGINA WILLIS, born 1910-12-1.

118

WALTON LAWRENCE (6) HAMPTON, (Solomon E. 5, Cary 4, John 3, John 2, Joseph 1), born near Milton, Ky., 1882-10-7. Educated first in graded schools of Carroll Co., Ky. Graduated by Madison, Ind. High School, in 1900. Going into business for himself, he tended his father's farm two years. Then engaged in work with the National Biscuit Co., at Minneapolis, Minn., at Evansville, Ind., and now (Jan., 1910), their superintendent at Salt Lake City, Utah. Member of the Methodist Episcopal Church South.

Politically, he says: "I am an American at Salt Lake."

Appendix

(Jersey Hamptons)

The matter contained in this appendix was not received by the editor till after the manuscript of the main body of the work was in the hands of the publisher. The existence of the persons was not known to the editor till afterwards.

FOURTH GENERATION.

1 BENJAMIN (4) HAMPTON, (Benjamin 3, Benjamin 2, Joseph 1), was the third child in the list of nine children of Benjamin 3, who married MARGARET POWELL (or POWNELL), as recorded on page 12.

He was born 1790-9-15, at Wrightstown, Bucks Co., Penn. Married HANNAH MORRIS, at Wrightstown, who was born 1791-4-30, and died 1844-1-16. They lived at Wrightstown, till their five sons were nearly grown and and then moved to Quakertown, New Jersey. He was a farmer and also a cabinet and a chair maker. In religion a strict Friend. Outlived his wife over 25 years and died 1869-10-31. Had his home over 20 years with his son, William.

Children:

I MORRIS, born 1817, ?, died 1903-8-7, 86 2-3 years.
II JOHN T., born 1823-4-2, died 1898-1-2, 74 3-4 years.
III WILLIAM WHARTON, born 1826-2-1, died 1885-2-11.
IV JAMES, born 1819-5-11.
V JOSEPH, born 1829-1-7, died March, 1900.

2. CATHARINE (4) HAMPTON, daughter of Benja-

min (3) Hampton, Jr., who married Margaret Powell (or Pownell), was the last in the list and probably the youngest of his nine children. Married HIRAM BURGISS. A son named Hampton Burgis, was killed by a bull. A daughter born after husband's death, was named Hampton Etta.

FIFTH GENERATION.

MORRIS (5) HAMPTON, (Benjamin 4, Benjamin 3, Benjamin 2, Joseph 1), born 1817, died 1903-8-7, age 86 2-3 years.

Married AMY HAMPTON CLIFTON, 1842-11-12, born 1815-6-29, and died 1885-7-27. She was the daughter of Wm. Clifton and Amy (Hampton) Clifton. After her marriage she called herself Amy Clifton Hampton.

He was a man of sterling qualities and respected by all who knew him and had considerable property. Was of the last members of the old Quaker meeting at Quakertown, N. J. "His place during service was on the bench back of the speakers platform. His nephew who is not a Quaker, says." "This may be assumed to mean in Quaker parlance, that he was an elder in the church and sat in the elder's gallery." Retained his mental faculties up to the time of his death. Farmer. Republican.

Children of Morris and Amy:

I REBECCA CLIFTON HAMPTON, born 1844-1-14, died 1857-8-29.
II WILLIAM CLIFTON HAMPTON, born 1845-8-25, died 1876-2-4.
III SARAH ELIZABETH HAMPTON, born 1847-9-11, died 1897-5-22.

JOHN T. (5) HAMPTON, (Benjamin 4, Benjamin 3, Benjamin 2, Joseph 1), born 1823-4-2, died 1898-1-2, age 74 3-4 years. Married Lucy Bray, to whom his property was left and who lived a few years after her husband's death. No children, Republican, Farmer, Friend.

WILLIAM WHARTON (5) HAMPTON, (Benjamin 4, Benjamin 3, Benjamin 2, Joseph 1), born 1826-2-1, in Bucks Co., Penn., died 1885-2-11, at Quakertown, N. J. Educated in public schools. Married SUSAN BALDWIN, 1847-3-20, born 1827-11-1, and educated in common schools. Died 1884-9-1. Both Methodists.

Children:

I HANNAH MARIA, born 1849-12-31.
II STEWART C., born 1854-3-22.
III JOSEPH ELROD, born 1856-3-17.
IV ANNA REBECCA, born 1863-2-7.
V WM. JUDSON, born 1866-4-1.
VI ALICE LULU, born 1868-3-3, died 1890-4-1.

JAMES (5) HAMPTON (Benjamin 4, Benjamin 3, Benjamin 2, Joseph 1), born 1819-5-11. Educated at Wrightstown, Pa., married MARY TITMAN, 1840-11-21, at Greenwood, Pa. She was born at Greenwood, Pa., 1823-12-21, and is still living, October, 1910. James died 1889-7-13. He was a contractor and builder. In religion, a Friend. A Sunday School teacher and active in church work. Supt. of Sunday School at Greenwood. Republican.

Children:

I DANIEL BALTIS, born 1841-9-12, at Quakertown, N. J.

II BENJAMIN MORRIS, born 1843-3-4, at Greenwood, Penn.

III HANNAH JANE, born 1845-8-28, at Greenwood, Pa., and died 1859-2-20, at Millville, Pa., aged 13 years, 5 months and 22 days.

IV ELIZABETH ABI, born 1849-10-2, at Greenwood,

Pa., died at Millville, Pa., 1857-2-4, aged 7 years, 4 months and 2 days.

V MARY ELEANOR, born 1851-6-26, at Greenwood, Pa.

VI LAURA ANN, born 1856-4-15, at Greenwood, Pa., died 1862-8-18, at Ashland, Pa., aged 6 years, 4 months and 3 days.

VII CARRIE REBECCA, born 1867-5-17, at Ashland, Pa.

JOSEPH HAMPTON, (Benjamin 4, Benjamin 3, Benjamin 2, Joseph 1), born ——, died March, 1900. Married MARY————.

He was a wagon-maker. They had one child, Mary Hampton, who married ———— Bond. Both now deceased. (A. D. 1910.) Joseph was a Republican.

SIXTH GENERATION.

SARAH ELIZABETH (6) HAMPTON, (Morris 5, Benjamin 4, Benjamin 3, Benjamin 2, Joseph 1), born 1847-9-11, married 1870-11-12, GEORGE DILLWYN LEAVER. Both now deceased (1910). She died 1897-5-22.

Children of Sarah Elizabeth (Hampton) Leaver:

1. MORRIS HAMPTON LEAVER, born 1872-6-22, M. D., D. D. S., is a prominent physician of Quakertown, N. J. His religious bent is toward the Quaker faith. Practicing both medicine and dentistry.

II WILLIAM LEAVER, born 1880-1-25.

III ALBERT ALLEN LEAVER, born 1883-4-15.

IV AMY LUCY LEAVER, born 1886-6-5.

V LUCY MAY LEAVER, born 1892-1-31.

HANNAH MARIA (6) HAMPTON, (William Wharton 5, Benjamin 4, Benjamin 3, Benjamin 2, Joseph 1), born

1849-12, at Quakertown, N. J. Married John S. Robinson, 1876-6-3. He was born 1847-8-15. Hannah is a Methodist.

Child of Hannah Maria: Earl Hapmton Robinson, born 1887-1-27. A farmer.

STEWART C. (6) HAMPTON, (William Wharton 5, Benjamin 4, Benjamin 3, Benjamin 2, Joseph 1), born 1854-3-22, at Quakertown, N. J. Married PHEBE R. SHAY, 1879-3-26, and died 1881-4-22. Merchant and a highly respected member of the Methodist church. Lived at Frenchtown, N. J.

Child: Nina Stewart Hampton, born 1881-2-18, at Frenchtown, N. J.

JOSEPH ELROD (6), (William Wharton 5, Benjamin 4, Benjamin 3, Benjamin 2, Joseph 1), born 1856-3-17, at Quakertown, N. J. Educated in public schools. Married MARY C. HOFF, 1881-7-20, at Baptisttown, N. J. She was born 1862-12-7.

"Reside about two miles from Baptisttown, N. J., on an excellent farm. He has always taken an interest in politics and voted the Republican ticket. His party has honored him with the nomination for County Clerk and for Member of Assembly, but the county being strongly Democratic, he was not elected. He polled a strong vote in both instances.

"Has also been interested in religious matters. Was connected with the Methodist Episcopal church." United with his wife who was a Baptist, in the Kingwood Baptist church. For 16 years he served the church as Sunday School Superintendent and for a number of years as Deacon and Church Clerk.

Child: Abijah Elrod Hampton, born 1882-10-27.

WILLIAM JUDSON (6) HAMPTON, (William Wharton 5, Benjamin 4, Benjamin 3, Benjamin 2, Joseph 1), born 1866-4-1, at Quakertown, N. J. Educated in public schools, Trenton Business College, Pennington Seminary and marticulated in Wesleyan University, but health failed in Freshman year. Later pursued studies in connection with Columbia, Taylor and New York Universities and Gale College. Honorary degree of Doctor of Divinity conferred by Taylor College in 1908. Converted in and joined the Baptist church, March, 1885, but left within six months and joined the Methodist Episcopal, Aug. 1st, 1885, at Quakertown, N. J., the church home of his parents. Licensed to preach Jan. 9th, 1888. Admitted to the Newark Annual Conference, 1892, at Morristown, N. J. Ordained Deacon in 1892, by Bishop Bowman, and Elder by Bishop Foss, in 1896. His appointments have been: Sparrowbush, N. J., Oxford, N. J., Succassana, N. J.; Grace Church, Dover, N. J., Chatham, N. J., Blairstown, N. J., Rockaway, N. J., Englewood, N. J., Bayonne, N. J., Forty-Sixth Street, Belvidere, N. J. Married AMELIA BOYCE, 1892-12-21, daughter of John A. and Julia Webb Boyce, and born 1863-6-20, at Monroe, N. J. Educated in public schools and in Newburg Institute, N. J.

Children:

I DELVON, born 1893-12-13, died 1884-8-7.
II WM. JUDSON, JR., born 1895-1-1.
III MARIE, born 1896-6-8, died 1896-7-26.
IV VERNON BOYCE, born 1897-6-26.
V EDITH MIRIAM, born 1901-7-10.
VI JAMES WEBB, born 1908-2-5.

Dr. Hampton has written several articles for the press. Also three booklets: Viz. History of Chatham, N. J. Methodist Episcopal Church; History of Forty-Sixth Street Methodist Episcopal Church, Bayonne, N. J., and The Paladian of Correct Morals.

ANNA REBECCA (6) HAMPTON, (William Wharton 5, Benjamin 4, Benjamin 3, Benjamin 2, Joseph 1), born 1863-2-7. Educated in public schools. Married JEREMY M. BURROUGHS, 1881-9-28. He is a mechanic.

DANIEL BALTIS (6) HAMPTON, (James 5, Benjamin 4, Benjamin 3, Benjamin 2, Joseph 1), born 1841-9-12, at Quakertown, N. J. Educated at Millville Seminary, Pa. Was a teacher. Also a soldier in the Civil War and honorably discharged because of illness. Married MARY MARGARET DRUMM, 1863-5-17, at Winfield, Penn. She was born at Lewisburg, Pa., 1844-1-31. He is a Methodist, a Sunday School teacher and active in church work. Living at Jamestown, N. J. Republican.

Children:

I BENJAMIN FREEMAN, born 1864-3-15, at Ashland, and died there in 1865-4-4.

II EMMA ELEANOR, born 1867-1-28, at Girardville, Pa., and died 1871-3-22, at Ashland, Penn.

III RACHEL ALVERNA, born 1869-10-1, at Jerseytown, Pa.

BENJAMIN MORRIS (6) HAMPTON, (James 5, Benjamin 4, Benjamin 3, Benjamin 2, Joseph 1), born 1843-3-4, at Greenwood, Pa. Educated in public schools. Married ELIZA GINDER TUNIS, 1867-10-13, at Girardville, Pa. She was born 1850-6-13, in Philadelphia, Pa., and educated in Philadelphia public schools.

The greater part of his life was spent at Ashland, Pa., where he was one of the influential business men of the place, being in the wholesale and retail flour and feed business.

He was a Methodist and a trustee of the church at Ashland. His home was called the "minister's home" entertaining visiting ministers including Presiding Elders in nearly all their visits. He was considered a very charitable man. Moved to Brookline, N. Y., in May, 1886, where he was a lumber merchant and a dealer in real estate and became a member of Hanson Place Methodist Church. Died 1889-12-9. Republican. No children. His widow married John Perry Williams, 1896-1-29, a

Vestryman in the Episcopal Church and a real estate dealer. Democrat.

MARY ELEANOR (6) HAMPTON, (James 5, Benjamin 4, Benjamin 3, Benjamin 2, Joseph 1), born 1851-6-26, at Greenwood, Pa. Educated in Pennsylvania Public Schools. Was teacher of the Bible Class of the Episcopalian Sunday School and active in the work of her own church, the Presbyterian and a teacher in its Sunday School. Married GEORGE SPARKS KEIPER, at Ashland, Pa., 1867-10-29. He was born at Akron, O., 1843-12-1. Educated at Allentown, Penn. Academy.

Was one of the first 530 Pennsylvania Volunteers who answered the first call of Abraham Lincoln for troops. Arrived at Washington, April 18th, 1861. Enlisted in "Three Months Service," and was honorably discharged July 18th, 1861. Re-enlisted Aug. 25th, 1862, for three years and was honorably discharged Apr. 13th, 1865. He Joined the Masons 1868. Was elected Master and went as high as thirtieth degree. Knight Templar. Appointed Postmaster at Ashland, Pa., for four years, Feb. 19th, 1890. School director six years at Ashland. Profession Dentistry. Later opened one of the finest jewelry stores in Ashland. Considered an expert jeweler. Retired from business 1910. Presbyterian and was Superintendent of Sunday School. Republican.

Children of Eleanor (Hampton) Keiper:

I GEORGE REUBEN KEIPER, born 1868-10-3, at Ashland, Pa., and died there 1869-6-16.

II MARY GERTRUDE KEIPER, born 1870-3-23. Educated in public schools and studied art in Ashland, Pa. Attended the New England Conservatory at Boston, Mass. Was organist in Presbyterian Sunday School and prayer meeting for 5 years. 1 1-2 years in English Luthern Church and 1 year in the Methodist Church in Ashland, Pa. After moving to Brooklyn, she was organist of the Arlington Avenue Presbyterian Church for over 9 years and for 14 years a member of the Executive Committee of the Ladies Aid Association of the same church.

She married Samuel Boyle Van Buren, 1895-11-28. He graduated at Pottsville, Pa., public schools. Took private lessons in cutting in New York City. Business: Commercial salesman. Member of the Musical and Literary Cotorie. Member of the Presbyterian Social Union. Elder in the Arlington Avenue Presbyterian Church of Brooklyn, N. Y. Republican. No children.

III BENJAMIN HAMPTON KEIPER, D. O. S., born 1872-9-1, in Ashland, Pa. Attended Ashland public schools, also American Horogical Institute in 1892, was considered a fine engraver. He also graduated from the South Bend College of Ophies in 1904. Married 1st, Cora Myrth Godshall in Jersey City, 1896-10-31. She was born 1879-4-1, in Caltawissa, Pa., and died 1898-10-9, in Brooklyn, N. Y. No children. Married 2nd, Cecelia Agnes Mosbach, 1905-2-15, (?), in Brooklyn, N. Y., who was born there 1877-2-8. She was educated in St. Joseph's Academy of Flushing, Long Island. Benjamin is a Presbyterian. Republican.

Children of Benjamin Keiper:

1. MARY GERTRUDE KEIPER, born 1905-6-29, in New Rochell, N. Y.
2. VINCENT ALOYSIUS KEIPER, born 1906-9-22, in Brooklyn, N. Y., and died there 1907-1-12.

IV CAROLINE ELIZA KEIPER, born 1877-12-5, in Ashland, Pa., and died there in 1880-2-20.

V ELLA LULU KEIPER, born 1883-3-20, in Ashland, Penn.

Educated in public schools of Ashland. Is a Presbyterian. Was married to HARRY RAY BROAD, 1905-8-15. He was born in Brooklyn, N. Y., 1878-11-2. No children. Mr. Broad is a veteran having served five years in the 13th National Guards of New York. He was educated in the

Polytechnic Institute. Joined the Masons in 1904. Presbyterian. Republican.

CARRIE REBECCA (6) HAMPTON, (James 5, Benjamin 4, Benjamin 3, Benjamin 2, Joseph 1), born 1867-5-17, at Ashland, Pa. Educated in Ashland public schools and at Bloomburg State Normal College. Also studied art in New York.

She was President of the Woman's Auxilliary of the 26th Ward, (Brooklyn) Branch, Y. M. C. A., for two years, Treasurer of the Woman's Council of the Y. M. C. A. Auxilliary, for the last three years and at present (Oct. 1910) also Secretary of the Woman's Auxilliary of the 26th Ward Branch Y. M. C. A., and a member of the Executive Board of the L. I. Council of Woman's Clubs. A member of one of the best and the largest Woman's clubs of Brooklyn, "The Chiropean." For two years corresponding secretary of the Arlington Avenue Presbyterian church Ladies Aid Society. Historian for two years of the Brooklyn Society of Mineral Painters. Now (Oct., 1910) President of the Friend In Need Day Nursery Association. At Brooklyn, N. Y., 1887-10-27, married to JOHN CONNER CREVELING born 1863-6-30, at Blooms-Pa. Educated in Columbia County, Pa., public schools and at Bloomsburg State Normal College. "After leaving school he clerked in the Produce Exchange for five years. Was then made manager, which position he resigned to go to Brooklyn, N. Y., where he is now (1910) in business as a lumber merchant and a manufacturer of doors, sash, blinds, mouldings, etc.

He is Secretary of the local School Board of District No. 40 of New York, a member of the Knights of St. John of Malta and Royal Arcanum. Member of the Penn. Grange Patron of Husbandry. Chairman of the Finance Committee of the 26th Ward Brooklyn, Y. M. C. A., a Trustee of the New York Lumber Trade Association. A member of the Trade Relations Committee. Member of the Executive Committee of the Brooklyn Presbyterian Union. Charter member, Elder and President of the

Board of Trustees of the Arlington Avenue Presbyterian Church. Member of the Musical and Literary Cotorie. Director of the Homestead Bank of Brooklyn, N. Y. Republican.

Children of Carrie R. (Hampton) Creveling:

I HAMPTON BENJAMIN CREVELING, born 1889-9-20, in Brooklyn, N. Y., and died there 1892-3-13.
II EMERSON DEL ROY CREVELING, born 1893-10-1, in Brooklyn, N. Y. Attending Pennington Seminary at Pennington, N. Y., in autumn of 1910.
III CLEOLAS CONNER CREVELING, born 1899-1-1, in Brooklyn, N. Y., died 1905-3-1, at West Palm Beach, Florida. His body was brought home and interred at Brooklyn.

SEVENTH GENERATION.

RACHEL ALVERNA (7) HAMPTON, (Daniel Baltis 6, James 5, Benjamin 4, Benjamin 3, Benjamin 2, Joseph 1), born 1869-10-1, at Jerseytown, Pa. Attended high school at Ashland and Shamokin, Pa., and Art School at New York City, Philadelphia, Pa., and Buffalo, N. Y. Married to WM. EDWARD KLUMBACH, 1891-5-28. She was president of Y. M. C. A. Auxilary two years at Jamestown, N. Y., her present home (1910). Methodist. Her husband, Wm. E. Klumbach, born 1867-4-29, at Utica, N. Y. Attended English and German schools there and graduated from the Mitchel Cutting School, N. York City, and is now (1910) a custom cutter at Jamestown, N. Y. He was on the Board of Directors, also Secretary of the Board of the Y. M. C. A., at Shomokin, Penn. Republican. Methodist.

Children of Rachel Alverna:

HAMPTON ROSCOE KLUMBACH, born 1893-12-20, at Shamokin, Pa. Attending High School at Jamestown, N. Y. (1910.)

NINA STEWART (7) HAMPTON, (Stewart C. 6, William Wharton 5, Benjamin 4, Benjamin 3, Benjamin 2, Joseph 1), born 1871-2-18, at Frenchtown, N. J. Married ELESTUS SHINER COLE, 1902-12-24.

Children of Nina Stewart (Hampton) Cole:

I KENNETH HAMPTON COLE.
II RALPH STEWART COLE.

Nina and Electus are Methodists. He is a teacher in public schools and a Democrat.

ABIJAH ELROD (7) HAMPTON, (Joseph Elrod 6, Wm. Wharton 5, Benjamin 4, Benjamin 3, Benjamin 2, Joseph 1), born 1882-10-27. Married Myrtle May Van Dorn, 1909-12-1.

Utah Hamptons

1 GRANT HAMPTON, of Salt Lake City, Utah, reports that his great grandfather Joseph Hampton was born about 1785, "evidently in Bucks County, Pennsylvania, where the family settled before the revolutionary war." That according to the testimony of his (Grant's) Aunt Mary Hampton Godbe, this Joseph Hampton married Mary Rummidge and that he was a Methodist.

Undoubtedly this Joseph was a descendent of "Joseph Hampton, from England," who settled at Wrightstown, Bucks county, Pennsylvania, and married Mary Canby, but through which of that Joseph's two sons Benjamin or John (known in this history as Benjamin 2, or John 2, because they were of the second generation of American Hamptons) does his lineage run?

If we can find the names of the parents of this Joseph born 1785) the answer will be easy.

According to our records there were four Joseph Hamptons born among the descendents of "Joseph from England," during the last half of that century, or between 1750 and 1800: 1st Joseph 3, son of John 2, born 17th of 8th month, 1753, who married Mary Blaker and settled in Catawissa. 2nd, Joseph the fourth child in the list of eleven children of this couple. The language of the record of their marriage and settlement at Catawissa, certainly indicates an early removal, and it is hardly possible that this fourth child should have been born before their going there. He must have been born a hundred miles or more away from Bucks county.

3rd, Joseph only son of David 3, son of John 2. He must, it seems, have been the Quaker preacher Hampton, from Pennsylvania, cousin of Asenath (Hampton) Doan who visited her at her home in Athens county, Ohio, in the fall of 1850, because he evidently was the only male cousin of the Hampton surname living in far eastern Pennsylvania, at that time.

John 2 had four sons: 1st, Joseph 3, whose family had gone to Catawissa, sixty or seventy years before. 2nd, Jonathan, whose family all seem to have been in Ohio many years.

3rd, her father, John 5, who had taken his family to Maryland, in 1801, and to Ohio in 1825, leaving, so far as we now know only David's family, himself, wife and one son (Joseph) and two daughters, in far eastern Pennsylvania. Thus it seems hardly possible that Joseph born about 1785, who became the ancestor of the Utah Hamptons could have been a descendent of John.

4th. But there was a fourth Joseph descended from Benjamin 2. He was the fourth child of Benjamin 3, who married Margaret Powell (or Pownell). The name Benjamin recurring so many times among his descendants is very significant. If this Joseph is the greatgrandfather of Grant Hampton, of Salt Lake City, his father and grandfather were both named Benjamin and he had a brother Benjamin who became the ancestor of the Jersey Hamptons who had their seat at Quakertown, Huntingdon county, New Jersey. And it is not surprising that he should have a son and a grandson Benjamin and a great-grandson Horace Benjamin.

The name John occurs in every generation of the descendents of John 2, but no Benjamin except Benjamin Franklin named for Franklin, the philosopher and statesman, in the fifth generation, so far as our records show. Assuming this view to be correct, this Joseph's lineage may be briefly written as follows:

JOSEPH (4) HAMPTON, (Benjamin 3, Benjamin 2, Joseph 1), born about 1785, in Bucks county, Pennsylvania, married Mary Rummidge. He was a Methodist. Probably a farmer and lived in Chester county, Pennsylvania.

Children of Joseph and Mary Cambridge Hampton:

I BENJAMIN, born 1810-6-18.

II HANNAH, married an Arnold.

III REBECCA, married a McCoy.

IV THOMAS.

V HORATIO, born on the China Sea. A sailor and unmarried.

2 BENJAMIN (5) HAMPTON, born 1810-6-18, on a farm in Chester county, Pennsylvania. Married at Philadelphia, Patience Schull, of a Quaker family and born at Woodbury, New Jersey. They lived a while at Philadelphia, but moved to Saint Louis, in 1845, and to Salt Lake City, in 1853. Family all Christians. Husband of Methodist family and wife of Quaker family.

Children:

I BENJAMIN (6), born 1837-2-11.

II MARY.

III ANNA.

IV ELVA.

3 THOMAS (5) HAMPTON, (Joseph 4, Benjamin 3, Benjamin 2, Joseph 1, born probably in Chester county, Pennsylvania. About 1845, moved to Buffalo, N. Y., and died there. Wife's name Catherine ——————. He was a plumber by trade.

BENJAMIN (6) HAMPTON, (Benjamin 5, Joseph 4, Benjamin 3, Benjamin 2, Joseph 1), born at Philadelphia, Penn., 1837-2-11, married at Salt Lake City, 1864-1-30,

Adelade E. Grant. She died 1895-2-16, aged 49 years. They lived at Salt Lake City.

His son writes: "My father was one of the first men in Utah to enter the mining business. Built smelters at Rush Lake, Utah, and at T———, Utah. Both were profitable. Lost a lot of money in developing a big placer gold mining property at Osceola, Nevada. Is now (March 1911) largest owner in the biggest deposit of antimony ore yet discovered. Located at Coyote Canyon, near Marysvale, Utah. Is a Christian Scientist. Still living March 20, 1911.

Children of Benjamin and Adelade Hampton:

I ADELADE, born 1864-11-7, at Salt Lake, unmarried.

II GRANT, born 1867-7-8, at Salt Lake City.

III WILLIAM YOULET, born 1870-3-11, at Bear River, Utah.

IV HORACE BENJAMIN, born 1872-8-19, at Bear River, Utah.

V ROBERT ROY, born 1875-5-19, at Bear River, Utah.

VI JOSEPH EUGENE, born 1877-10-7, at Salt Lake City, and died there 1877-12-1.

MARY (6) HAMPTON, (Benjamin 5, Joseph 4, Benjamin 3, Benjamin 2, Joseph 1), born in Philadelphia, Penn. Educated in public schools in St. Louis, Mo. Moved to Salt Lake City, in 185-?, married there to William Samuel Godbe, 1856-11-10. Her daughter, Mrs. Miriam G. Brooks, reports the mother's early life as uneventful; but adds "Mary Hampton Godbe's subsequent life forms one of the important events in the history of Utah, she being the first woman to come out openly against the depotism of the Mormon church.

"This epoch in Utah's history is known as the Godbeite movement, named after William S. Godbe who organized it in 1870 and was the beginning of a bitter warfare against the Mormon church which has continued ever since," March, 1911. Mrs. Godbe is still living at this date, not in fellowship with any church. In politics her sympathy is with the Republicans.

Children:

I MILLICENT ANN GODBE, born 1860-4-6, at Salt Lake City, and died there 1889-9-27. Married Charles P. Brooks, of New York, 1876-9-28.

Children:

I CLARA GODBE BROOKS, born 1879-12-5, at Salt Lake City, married James Henry Pitts, 1902-7-2, at Salt Lake City.

Children:

1. WINNEFRED PITTS, born 1903-11-20, at Salt Lake City.
2. JEAN PITTS, born 1909-5-12, Salt Lake City.

II MIRIAM BROOKS, born 1885-4-2, at Salt Lake City.

III MARJORIE BROOKS, born 1888-9-28, at Salt Lake City, married LEVI JENNINGS, 1910-6-8, at Salt Lake City.

II ANTHONY HAMPTON GODBE, born 1862-11-22, at Salt Lake City, married RUBY ———, Sept. 15, 1898.

Children:

1. VIRGINIA GODBE, born 1899-12-13, at Salt Lake City.

3. MARGARET GODBE, born 1901-6-18, at Salt Lake City.

3. HAMPTON GODBE, born 1906-5-2, at Salt Lake City.

III MIRIAM GODBE, born 1865-6-1, at Salt Lake City, married CHARLES F. BROOKS, husband of deceased sister, 1901-12-15. Salt Lake City. No children.

IV ERNEST LACY GODBE, born 1867-9-15, at Salt Lake City, married Sallie Werthheimer, January, 1888.

Children:

I VIOLA GODBE, born 1889-6-6, at Pioche, Nevada, married to Emile E. Werk, of Cincinnati, O., at Salt Lake City, 1909-9-15.

2. MILLICENT GODBE, born 1890-8-12, at Pioche, Nevada.

3. BERTHA GODBE, born 1892-9-7, at Pioche, Nev.

4. MIRIAM GODBE, born 1895-5-18, at Pioche, Nev.

5. BENJAMIN HAMPTON GODBE, born 1887-4-19, at Salt Lake City.

6. WILLIAM BRIAN GODBE, born 1899-12-25, at Salt Lake City.

7. LILLIAN GODBE, born 1903-4-5.

8. JACK GODBE, born 1906-7-5.

9. ERNEST LACY GODBE, born 1908-9-17.

V MURRAY CHARLES GODBE, born 1870-9-20, at Salt Lake city. Married Alta Young, 1892-3-17, at Salt Lake City.

Children:

1. RUTH GODBE, born 1893-1-14, at Salt Lake City.

2. MARY HAMPTON GODBE, born 1895-9-28, at Salt Lake City.

3. HELEN GODBE, born 1898-7-12, at Ogden, Utah.

4. MURRAY C. GODBE, born 1901-6-23, at Salt Lake City, Utah.

VI ELVA BERSTOCK GODBE.

She is the child of Mary Hampton Godbe's youngest sister, Elva Hampton, who married a Mr. Berstock and adopted by her aunt Mary and husband Wm. S. Godbe, born 1874-2-11, at Morgan, Utah, married Patrick Shehan, 1900-4-18, at Salt Lake City.

Children:

1. ALICE SHEHAN, born 1901-12-31, at De Lamar, Nevada.

2. DANIEL SHEHAN, born 1905-1-1, at Stateline, Utah.

3. PATRICK SHEHAN, born 1908-2-6, at Salt Lake City.

4. BENJAMIN HAMPTON SHEHAN, born 1910-9-27, at Salt Lake City.

ANNA (6) HAMPTON, (Benjamin 5, Joseph 4, (?) Benjamin 3, (?), Benjamin 2, (?), Joseph 1), born in Pennsylvania, in 1840. Married to Rynaldo Mowry at Salt Lake City, in 1856. She died at Salt Lake City, Jan. 12th, 1898. He died May 5th, 1906.

Children of Anna H. Mowry:

I RUTH W. MOWRY, born 1858-10-12, at Salt Lake City. Married to James G. Bywater, 1878-11-24, at Salt Lake City.

Children of Ruth W. Mowry.

1. JOSEPH FRANK BYWATER, born 1879-7-20, at Logan City, Utah. He married Suda Jones, 1902-10-28, at Salt Lake City.

Children:

1. LAWRENCE BYWATER, born 1903-12-5, at Salt Lake City.

2. GLEUN (?) BYWATER, born Jan., 1906, at Salt Lake City.

3. LAMAR (?) BYWATER, born May, 1908, at Salt Lake City.

4. WILLIAM (?) BYWATER, born July, 1909 at Salt Lake City.

2. RUTH ELSIE BYWATER, born 1882-4-25, at Logan City, Utah. She was married to Joseph M. Gorgensen, at Salt Lake City, June 12th, 1903.

Children:

1. JOSEPH NORMAN GORGENSEN, born 1904-5-31.

2. RUTH REAVE GORGENSEN, born 1908-3-4.

3. MURRY N. BYWATER, born 1884-7-22, at Logan City, Utah.

4. GEORGE G. BYWATER, born 1886-4-1, at Logan City, Utah.

5. JANET B. BYWATER, born 1889-1-21, at Logan City, Utah.

6. LYNN G. BYWATER, born 1893-8-28, at Salt Lake City, Utah.

7. GLADYS A. BYWATER, born 1900-2-7, at Salt Lake City, Utah.

II ANNA AMELIA MOWRY, born 1860-12-27, married to Thomas B. Margetts, Aug., 1880.

Children:

1. CATHARINE ANNA MARGETTS, born 1881-5-14, at Salt Lake City. Married to Albert E. Stanley, 1907-9-11, at Salt Lake City.
Child: Lewis Vernon, born 1908-8-11, at Salt Lake City.

2. MYRTH AVONAL MARGETTS, born 1883-7-27, married to Albert C. Gondry, 1907-6-26, at Salt Lake City.

3. EMMA LEVERNE MARGETTS, born 1886-6-18, at Salt Lake City, married Frederick T. Gundry, 1906-8-23, at Salt Lake City.
Child: Ardis LeVerne Gundry, born 1910-4-26, at Salt Lake City.

4. RICHARD B. MARGETTS, born 1888-10-22, at Salt Lake City, married Juanita Hellstrom, 1909-10-11, at Salt Lake City.
Child: Cyril Hampton Margetts, 1910-7-27.

III EMMA DELTA MOWRY, born 1862-10-6, at Lake City, married to Dewoody R. Jones, Nov., 1882, at Salt Lake City.

Children:

1. ARTHUR MOWRY JONES, born Sept., 1883, at Salt Lake City.

2. ETHYL JONES, born Feb. 29, 1888, at Seattle, Wash. Married to Walter Sherman, June 26th, 1908, at Seattle, Wash.

3. EUGENE JONES, born 1890, at Seattle, Wash.

4. SHEREDON JONES, born 1892, at Seattle, Wash.

IV GRACE MOWRY, born 1864-8-17, died 1867-11-23, Salt Lake City.

V MARY MAY, born 1866-11-23, at Salt Lake City, married to Alexander Hyslop, 1883, Salt Lake City. He died 1910, (?), 12-23, at Provo, Utah.

Children:

1. LEON MOWRY HYSLOP, born 1884, at Salt Lake City, married Ida Kimpton, 1905, (?), at Pocatello, Idaho.

2. ERNEST HYSLOP, born 1887, at Salt Lake City.

3. ARTHUR HYSLOP, born 1890, at Salt Lake City.

4. DONALD HYSLOP, born 1899, at Pocatello, Idaho.

VI RHYNALDO MOWRY, Jr., born 1871-10-14, Salt Lake City, died 1880-1-14.

VII EFFIE MOWRY, born 1873-11-6, at Salt Lake City, married to Harry G. Junkin, 1896-9-22, at Salt Lake City.

VIII MYRTLE AVANOL MOWRY, born 1875-11-24, at Salt Lake City, married to JAMES FORSYTHE, 1895-6-26, at Salt Lake City.

Child: Eugene Forsythe, born 1897-2-28, at Portland, Oregon.

ELVA (6) HAMPTON, (Benjamin 5, Joseph 4, Benjamin 3, (?), Benjamin 2, Joseph 1), born at Salt Lake City, died 1874-2-19, at Littleton, Utah. Married DANIEL BERTOCH (or BUTOCH) 1866-11-24, at Salt Lake City.

Children of Elva:

I DANIEL HAMPTON BERTOCH (or Butoch), born 1868-8-19, at S. L. City.

II MARGUERITE BERTOCH (or Butoch), born 1870-8-28, at Littleton, Utah, died June, 1872, at Salt Lake City.

III JOHN BERTOCH (Butoch), born 1872-12-15, at Littleton, Utah, and died day of birth.

IV ELVA BERTOCH (or BUTOCH), born 1874-2-7, at Littleton, Utah. Adopted by her aunt, Mary Hampton Godbe.

Daniel Hampton Bertoch (or Butoch), No. 1 of the children, married Mary E. Kohlepp, Feb., 1905, at Logan, Utah.

Children:

1. ELVA, born 1906, at Pocatella, Idaho.
2. DANIEL, born 1907-10-11, at Pocatella, Idaho.

GRANT (7) HAMPTON, (Benjamin 6, Benjamin 5, Joseph 4, Benjamin 3, Benjamin 2, Joseph 1), born 1867-9-8, at Salt Lake City, married CATHERINE AURELIA LOWE, 1904-9-15, at Salt Lake City, Utah. Occupation March, 1911, Assistant Secretary and Treasurer and Director of the Consolidated Wagon and Machine Co., of Salt Lake, leading implement and vehicle dealers in Utah and Idaho.

Children:

I ANNA LOWE, born 1905-7-21, at Salt Lake City.

II AURDICE, born 1910-8-28, at Salt Lake City.

8 WILLIAM YOULET (7) HAMPTON, (Benjamin

5, Joseph 4, Benjamin 3, Benjamin 2, Joseph 1), born 1870-3-11, at Bear River, Utah, married at Salt Lake City, Utah, Hattie Lyman.

Children:

I CLARA LOUISE, born 1894-8-2, at Salt Lake City.

II ADELADE, born 1897-2-2, at Salt Lake City.

III LEONE, born 1902-6-10, at Salt Lake City.

V MARY, born 1905, at Odgen, Utah.

VI BENJAMIN, born 1910-3-4, at Ogden, Utah.

HORACE BENJAMIN (7) HAMPTON, (Benjamin6, Benjamin 5, Joseph 4, Benjamin 3, Benjamin 2, Joseph 1), born 1872-8-19, at Bear Creek, Utah, married Jean Pearson. He was killed by accident in a mill of the Silver King Mining Co., at Park City, Utah, died 1905-5-24.

Child:

1. ADELADE, born 1905-6-13, at Park City, Utah.

ROBERT ROY (7) HAMPTON, (Benjamin 6, Benjamin 5, Joseph 4, Benjamin 3, Benjamin 2, Joseph 1), born 1875-5-19, at Bear River, Utah, married 1900-12-29, at Salt Lake City, ELIZABETH HOWATT. A specialist physician in diseases of "eye, nose and throat." Had "thorough training in Chicago, New York and Germany."

Child:

1. Jane Grant, born 1904-1-11, at Salt Lake City.

Unclassified Hamptons

VAN CALEN HAMPTON, born in Salem Co., N. J., March 25th, 1799. He married (as his grandson, Benjamin Bowles Hampton, thinks) Elizabeth Randolph, born Aug. 30th, 1801. One of their sons, Benjamin Randolph Hampton, married Angeline Hall, daughter of Durham Hall, of Franklin Co., (their grandson thinks) Kentucky. They lived at McComb, Ill.

Children:

I DAVID HALL HAMPTON who married Mary Bowles, daughter of Henry Bowles, who had married Margaret Elizabeth Throop, of Evansville, Ind.
II WILLIAM RANDOLPH HAMPTON.
III DURHAM VAN CALEN HAMPTON.

Children of David Hall Hampton:

I BENJAMIN BOWLES HAMPTON, who married Maria Somers Bartleson, daughter of Horarito R. Bartleson, at McComb, Ill., Feb. 16th, 1898. They now (1911) live at Yonkers, New York. He is the editor of Hampton's Magazine.

Children of Benjamin B. and Maria S. Hampton:

I Catharine, 2 David Bartlison, 3 Helen Janet, 4 Mary Elizabeth, 5 Benjamin Randolph.

II LUCY ETHEL HAMPTON (daughter of David Hall) maried Stewart Donskin. They live at Minneapolis, Minn.

III JESSE DURHAM HAMPTON (son of David Hall) married Mable Harrison. Live in New York City. (1911).

EDITORIAL NOTE. The foregoing geneology of a family of American Hamptons was furnished by Mr. Benjamin B. Hampton, one of them, and the editor of Hampton's Magazine. In regard to their place among American Hamptons, two questions seem naturally to arise: First. Do they belong to the Pennsylvania or Northern family or are they descended from some branch of the Southern Hamptons? If the former from which of the two sons of the original Joseph, Benjamin or John do they come?

Without attempting to decide in a positive way these questions without more light, I very strongly incline to believe that the Van Calen Hampton who was born March 25th, 1799, in Salem Co., New Jersey, was a great grandson of Benjamin, son of the original "Joseph Hampton from England, who settled at Wrightstown, Bucks Co., Penn., and married Mary Canby, about the fall of 1722.

My reasons are: 1st, Salem Co., N. J., was near enough to Bucks Co., Penn., for some of the descendants to have gone there without great effort in moving. 2nd, The Hampton tradition in reference to the brothers of our great ancestor, Joseph, given me in childhood by my mother, as I now remember it, placed them farther south. 3rd, the christian name Benjamin, seems to continue among the descendents of Benjamin 2, as John does among the descendents of his brother John.

Because the Friends (Quakers) counted their children as church members and I believe always so enrolled them, it might be wise in any Hamptons who know or believe themselves to be descended from the Pennsylvania Hamptons, to search the records of the early "meetings" (churches) of the Friends of eastern Pennsylvania, for help to trace their lineage.

J. H. D.

Index
(Of Given Names)

Adda Achsa 94
Ann 6
Anna 47, 109
Ann P. 53
Adaline Adetia 69
Amos 29
Amy Alice 62
Asenath 4, 21, 59
Asa C 23
Benjamin 2, 7
Benjamin F. 38
Bethula 19
Bethula Ann 42
Bessie Payne 116
Cary 15, 17, 27
Caroline Asenath 65
Celia Annetta 64
Charles Henry 76
Charles Nevil 90
Chester Clyde 85
Clara Bell 77
Cora Bell 102
Clinton Elmer 104
Chester Larue 87
David 11
Daniel W. 82
Delwin 83
Edgar Clifton 86
Edward 50
Ella Alwilda 80
Ella Kate 115
Eli G. 39
Elizabeth 96
Eliza 48
Emily 57
Emma Lodiska 79
Ernest Elmer 78
Estella Victoria 70

Emlen 66
Frank Julius 91
Frank Julius 91
Frank A. 111
Gertrude 71
Hattie Annette 81
Harvey Moore 117
Ida 101
Isaac Steere 54
James 9, 20
John 3, 16, 24
James Hiram 32
James W. 40
James Elmer 63
Jesse 41
Jesse B. 18, 28
Jesse James 75
John Williamson 97
John Pierpoint 108
Joseph 1, 10, 106
Jeptha 92
Jonathan 12
Jonathan P. 51
Levi 30
Lindley 74
Lewis Pusey 68
Lovina 49
Lucinda 46
Lucinda M. 93
Mary 14, 31, 52
Mary Ann 26
Mary Eliza 57
Mary Delitha 88
Mary Elma 36
Mary Emily 113
Mary Jane 105
Martha 37
Mahalah Melvina 60
Maude 112
Moses Jackson 114
Nathan P. 61
Nettie 99
Oliver 8, 43
Oliver Asa 72
Richard B. 55
Robert W. 45
Ruth 34, 110

Sarah 5
Sarah G. 35
Sarah W. 44
Sarah C. 97
Samuel B. 25, 100
Solomon E. 58
Thomas 13
Thomas Elwood 95
Walter John 89
Walton Lawrence 118
William 33, 107
William Steere 66
William Allen 73
William Everett 103
Wilbur E. 84
Zachariah 22

Index

(Of Family Names)

Adams—91.
Allen—114-164.
Allison—123.
Armstrong—153.
Anderson—144.
Arnold—24-29.
Ashton—81.
Bailey—57-89-144.
Baker—13-132.
Bandy—161.
Ballard—88.
Barton—62.
Barns—149.
Barcroft—164.
Batty—55-78.
Bedell—83-85.
Beach—101.
Bond—157.
Bonar—150.
Bennett—91.
Bicksler—151.
Beals—156.
Billig—69.
Bixby—145.
Bundy—48-77-84-153.
Burns—164.
Blylock—148.
Burgess—67.
Booth—83.
Bowles—76.
Brown—146.
Betts—15-17.
Branch—90.
Briggs—75-158.
Bye—15-76.
Boswell—10.
Blakey—17.
Buffington—151.
Bentley—119.
Blacklege—123.
Benard—123.
Batchelder—128.
Blackburn—134.
Canby—5-17.
Cain—146.
Carbee—57.
Cary—15-16-17.
Calderwood—108.
Carlson—155.
Cope—81.
Cole—159.
Comly—9.
Clarke—159.
Coleman—8.
Croasdale—8.
Crumly—156.
Christy—137.
Clendenning—58.
Crew—83.
Coppeck—152.
Daugherty—156.
Day—163.
Davis—47-79-109.
Doan—11-31-87-133
Dodson—89.
Doudna—84-153.
Dathan—150.
DeWolf—149.
Duer—8.
Dunn—154.
Drane—107.
Deem—124.
Dull—98.
Dunfee—126.
Douglas—62.
Edgerton—81.

Eggleston—166.
Ellis—50-138.
Edmonson—159.
Elyson—153.
Engle—60.
English—91.
Embree—58-76.
Elliott—124.
Faucet—153.
Field—15.
Fisher—29.
Fogg—154.
Forbes—106.
Furguson—152.
Furney—164.
Farmer—83.
Gable—98.
Garber—166.
Gamble—154.
Gaston—63.
Germain—104.
Goodrich—102.
Gidley—88.
Gilbert—60.
Gordon—58.
Greek—103.
Griswald—63.
Griffith—33-34.
Gruver—145.
Gregg—73-77-150.
Geist—69.
Good—146.
Grewell—155.
Gould—115.
Groenveld—125.
Gad—128.
Hacket—49.
Hanks—87.
Hattes—150.
Hallowell—92.
Hazelrig—88.
Hiatt—160-162.
Heacock—155.
Hixon—157.
Highly—147.
Holden—145.
Hall—10-74-76-79.
Hays—107.
Hess—78.
Heald—159.
Hoyle—14.
Henderson—80.
Hazelton—78.
Hoagland—95.
Hansen—103.
Hurst—104.
Hughes—139.
Hirst—89.
Hodges—139.
Harmell—146.
Haycroft—127.
Howard—133.
Isham—66.
Irving—69.
Jarvis—3.
John—158.
Johnson—52-127.
Jones—156-157.
Judkins—138.
Kester—148.
Kitchen—12.
King—10-143.
Kirkpatrick—16-92.
Klugkist—125.
Kelley—131.
Lacy—16.
Lambert—146.
La Motte—145.
Lee—162.
Lee Braun—140.
Livzey—9.
Lownes—16.
Langstaff—60.
Mann—109.
McKie—109.
Martin—61.
Miller—159.
McKinley—93.
Millhouse—158.
Mott—10-39-74.
Moon—159.
Morrison—84.
Moore—96-122-124-152.
Merrill—147.

Marshall—111.
McAlister—114.
Macauley—120.
Mitchel—123.
McClure—123.
Morris—12-124.
Mendenhall—13.
Neal—131.
Nelson—155.
Newtin—75.
Newell—120.
Nuel—128.
Odle—93.
Olivere—111.
Outland—79.
Owens—143.
Palmer—61.
Parkerson—103.
Pederson—143.
Pemplin—88.
Patterson—10-35-49.
Pearson—57.
Phillips—13.
Pettyjohn—163.
Pierpoint—40.
Powell—12.
Poyner—52.
Parrill—91.
Plumly—31.
Pryor—167.
Prince—102.
Paxton—15.
Purnel—111.
Purviannce—129.
Pine—134.
Quinn—164.
Ray—161.
Rankin—102.
Rapp—92.
Regan—59.
Risser—72.
Robins—24-43-134.
Roman—10-13-14.
Rockwell—80.
Reed—111-121.
Rockway—125.
Rummidge—12.
Saunders—163.
Shannon—163.
Sothers—151.
Sharpless—160.
Shirk—139.
Sigler—106.
Sibert—164.
Shipman—63.
Smoleski—103.
Snyder—132.
Sprague—150.
Slaughter—107.
Stokes—7.
Spencer—60.
Swartwout—147.
Spear—86.
Stackhouse—17.
Slack—87-133.
Strite—154.
Smith—9-140-162.
Steer—40.
Stout—55.
Sphan—66.
Sheridan—160.
Stewart—111.
Shephard—119.
Shotwell—122.
Stanton—122.
Sherman—125.
Smally—127.
Simons—134.
Taylor—61.
Tedrow—68.
Test—153.
Tower—108.
Thornbury—123.
Tibals—127.
Tippy—132.
Trott—134.
Twiggs—135.
Vail—34-151.
Van Fleet—128.
Walker—17.
Watson—8.
Way—14.
Walters—109.
Warring—75.

Wells—90-91.
Welch—148.
Weeks—59.
Wilson—7-128.
Willis—167.
Winder—152.
Willetts—160.
Williamson—155.
Wire—88.
Whetstone—87.
Williams—38-88.
Wood—54.
Wildman—8.
Walton—30.
Webster—111.
Walden—129.
Whitnack—135.
Weiner—150.
West—73.
Yocum—158.
Young—75.